REVISION GUIDE

Official Publisher Partnership

OCR
INFORMATION and COMMUNICATION TECHNOLOGY
for A2

- Glen Millbery
- Sonia Stuart

HODDER
EDUCATION
AN HACHETTE UK COMPANY

The Publishers would like to thank the following for permission to reproduce copyright material:

Photo credits
Running head image © John Foxx/Imagestate Media; **p.22** © Gareth Leung/Fotolia;
p.23 *T* © Alex Segre/Alamy; **p.34** © Foto Factory/Alamy; **p.35** *L* © John Kershaw/Alamy;
R © Sahua D/Fotolia; **p.36** © Linleo/Fotolia; **p.42** © Stefano Maccari/Fotolia; **p.43** *T* © Daniel
Gale/Fotolia; *B* © Kevin Penhallow/Fotolia; **p.45** © Krysek/Fotolia; **p.46** *T* © titimel35/Fotolia;
B © ImageState/Alamy; **p.47** © Jeff Cleveland/Shutterstock; **p.50** © Tony French/Alamy;
p.51 *T* © Rainer Plendl/Fotolia; *M* © Stephen Finn/Fotolia; *B* © Eddie Gerald/Alamy;
p.55 © Henry Bonn/Fotolia; **p.60** © Heide Benser/Corbis; **p.66** *L* © Monkey Business/Fotolia;
R © VIEW Pictures Ltd/Alamy; **p.69** © Chuck Mason/Alamy; **p.80** © Superstars_for_You/
Fotolia; **p.89** © Jo Katanigra/Alamy

Acknowledgements
Microsoft product screenshots reprinted with permission from Microsoft Corporation;
p.23 *B* Photo © TomTom International BV, reproduced with permission; **p.48** Photo of
Spot GPS messenger reproduced with permission of Spot; **p.54** Photo of small computer
reproduced with permission of Archos

Every effort has been made to trace all copyright holders, but if any have been inadvertently
overlooked the Publishers will be pleased to make the necessary arrangements at the first
opportunity.

Although every effort has been made to ensure that website addresses are correct at time of
going to press, Hodder Education cannot be held responsible for the content of any website
mentioned in this book. It is sometimes possible to find a relocated web page by typing in
the address of the home page for a website in the URL window of your browser.

Hachette UK's policy is to use papers that are natural, renewable and recyclable products and
made from wood grown in sustainable forests. The logging and manufacturing processes are
expected to conform to the environmental regulations of the country of origin.

Orders: please contact Bookpoint Ltd, 130 Milton Park, Abingdon, Oxon OX14 4SB.
Telephone: (44) 01235 827720. Fax: (44) 01235 400454. Lines are open 9.00–5.00,
Monday to Saturday, with a 24-hour message answering service. Visit our website at
www.hoddereducation.co.uk

© Glen Millbery, Sonia Stuart 2010

First published in 2010 by

Hodder Education,

An Hachette UK Company

338 Euston Road

London NW1 3BH

Impression number   5 4 3 2 1

Year   2014 2013 2012 2011 2010

Cover photo © Ingram Publishing Limited

Illustrations by GreenGate Publishing Services

Typeset in ITC Stone Sans Medium 11pt by GreenGate Publishing Services, Tonbridge, Kent

Printed in Spain by GraphyCems

A catalogue record for this title is available from the British Library

ISBN: 978 1444 111231

Contents

Introduction

This book is not intended to be a text book that is used in class but is a revision guide that helps you prepare for your exam. It is a basic summary of the main points on which you will be assessed. It should be supplemented by notes that you make in class.

The revision guide follows the specification – each section contains a reference to the specification. The content is covered in either single pages or double-page spreads. To make life easier for you, all double-page spreads have been laid out on facing pages – this has sometimes meant that the lettering does not follow exactly the same order as the specification.

The revision guide is laid out with useful tips at the start of sections – these are things to look out for when answering questions on the topic. It has definitions and useful web links if you want to investigate a different aspect of the topic. The content itself has been reduced to the key points you need to know. However, this is a revision guide and although it tries to cover everything, it should be regarded as a supplement to your learning of the course.

There are questions at the end of each section and some items that you need to consider before answering questions on the topics covered. The questions are there to make you think about how the content will be applied in the examination. There are, of course, many other different questions you might be asked – these are not the only ones.

1 The systems cycle

1.1 Different approaches

Specification reference

3.3.1b – discuss different approaches an analyst might use when investigating a system: questionnaires, interviews, meetings, document analysis, observation.

 Key points to remember

- There are different methods of investigation that can be used to gather information.
- The analyst will select the most appropriate method of investigation based on people, type of information and the place in which information is being gathered.

Method	Benefits	Limitations
Questionnaires	▪ Large numbers of people can be asked the same questions, therefore comparisons are easy to make. ▪ Cheaper than interviews. ▪ Response can be anonymous.	▪ Must be designed very carefully. Questions need to be unambiguous. ▪ Cannot guarantee 100% return rate – may be lower with some groups.
Interviews	▪ A rapport can be developed with the people who will use the system. ▪ Questions can be adjusted or added as the interviews proceed.	▪ Can be time consuming and costly. ▪ It might not be possible to interview everyone.
Meetings	▪ A group of people can attend a meeting with different views being expressed. ▪ Can be used to gather or give information. ▪ Body language can be seen.	▪ The discussions can lose focus resulting in the questions not being fully answered. ▪ Some staff may not attend because jobs still need to be completed.
Document/record analysis and inspection	▪ Good for obtaining factual information.	▪ Cannot be used when input, output and information are not document-based.
Observation	▪ All aspects of work loads, methods of working, delays and 'bottlenecks' can be identified.	▪ Can be time consuming and costly. ▪ Problems may not occur during observation. ▪ Users may put on a performance when being observed.

Exam question

1 Discuss the use of interviews as an investigation method.
[*6 marks*]

Examiner hints and tips

Think about the following in relation to the question on the left.

The question refers to the use of interviews as an investigation method. You must focus your answer on interviews and provide the relevant benefits and limitations.

1.2 Stages of the system life cycle

Specification reference

3.3.1a – describe the following stages of the system life cycle (definition of the problem, investigation and analysis, design, implementation, testing, installation, documentation, evaluation and maintenance) and how the stages relate to ICT systems.

Keyword

System life cycle: the stages that need to be completed to create a new or modified system. Referred to as a cycle as, after time, the process will have to be repeated.

Key points to remember

- All projects should follow the system life cycle to ensure the final product fully meets the needs of the end user.
- The system life cycle is a continuous loop with each stage leading onto the next.

The **system life cycle** has no clear start or finish point as it is an iterative process. The most common start point is when a new software system is being considered.

Definition of the problem – the first stage of the system life cycle (also known as the feasibility stage). This is the initial look at the existing system to see how it can be improved or if it is possible to meet the needs and requirements of the end users. The analyst should also consider why a new system is required. For the project to continue, the new system must also be viable in terms of hardware and software choices, budget and time scale.

Investigation and analysis – this stage follows the definition of the problem and must be fully completed before moving to the design stage. Questionnaires, interviews, observations, meetings and document analysis can be used during this stage (see section 3.3.1b, on page 5). The results of the investigation are analysed to gain a full understanding of all the problems of the current system. The user requirements are defined and agreed with the client. These are constantly referred to during the development of the new system and form the basis for the rest of the system life cycle.

Design – the third stage of the system life cycle and comes after the investigation and analysis stage is completed. This stage must be concluded before the implementation stage is started. The objectives defined in the investigation and analysis stage are followed. The methods and formats of data capture, input, output, structure of data, processing and validation routines, queries and reports are all designed. The project plan is developed taking into account the client-defined deadline for the installation of the system.

Implementation – the fourth stage of the system life cycle (also known as the development stage). This stage is about taking the design forward and putting it into practice to build the system. A decision about the software strategy, based on budget constraints set by the client, is made. Coding, macros and queries are created with backup and storage of data being considered.

Testing – this stage comes after the implementation stage is completed. Testing follows a test plan, with results being recorded, and ensures that the system is free of bugs/errors and meets the defined user requirements. If a test fails to provide the expected result then corrective action is taken before a retest.

Installation – the system is installed for the client. The installation strategy is chosen (see sections 3.3.5d and 3.3.5e on pages 74–75) and training of the end users is carried out at this stage.

Documentation – the seventh stage of the system life cycle. Documentation, such as test plans, data and logs, user manuals, version and security details, and program specifications are created and passed to the user of the system.

Evaluation and maintenance – this is the final stage and may form the basis on which the decision is taken to begin the system life cycle again. This demonstrates the iterative nature of the system life cycle. The solution should be evaluated once it has been implemented with **maintenance** ensuring that a system continues to meet the needs of its users (see sections 3.3.5g and 3.3.5h on pages 77–78).

Stage	Input	Output
Definition of the problem		Feasibility study
Investigation and analysis	Feasibility study	Requirements specification
Design	Requirements specification	Designs
Implementation	Designs	Completed system
Testing	Completed system/test plans	Working system/test logs
Installation	Working system	Installed system

The inputs and outputs of stages in the system life cycle

Exam question

1 Describe the design and testing stages of the system life cycle.
[*8 marks*]

Examiner hints and tips

Think about the following in relation to the above question.

As you need to describe two stages of the system life cycle, you can assume that there are four marks allocated for each stage. You will need to consider the activities that occur within each stage, the inputs and outputs of each stage and the position of each stage within the system life cycle.

1.3

Software development methodologies

Specification reference

3.3.1c – describe the following software development methodologies: prototyping and rapid application development (RAD).

Keyword

Prototyping: a software development methodology which focuses on the early delivery to end users of an incomplete, but working, system which can then be changed following feedback from the client.

Key points to remember

■ The main methodology used when developing a software system is the system life cycle.

■ Other methodologies could be used, such as prototyping and rapid application development (RAD).

■ Prototyping

A prototype enables the end users to evaluate the proposals for the design of software by trying them out, rather than having to interpret and evaluate the design based on descriptions.

End users can find it difficult to define their exact requirements. **Prototyping** can be used to check that what the designer has created is what the end users want and need.

A prototype enables design options to be tried out and problems with possible solutions to be investigated.

There are two main types of prototyping: evolutionary and throw-away.

Evolutionary – an initial prototype is developed and evaluated by the end users. Using this feedback a second prototype is developed and then evaluated. This process continues with each prototype and evaluation making the system closer to what the end users require. Finally, on the last evaluation, the system should meet all the requirements.

Throw-away – a working model of various parts of the system is developed after a short investigation. The prototype is developed and evaluated by the end users but is not used in the final solution – it is thrown away! This enables the end users to give, and receive, quick feedback, which means that any refinements can be done early in the development. This is cost effective because there is nothing to redo. If a project is changed after considerable work has been done, then small changes could require large efforts to implement since software systems have many dependencies.

The benefits of prototyping include:

■ Reduced time and costs.

■ Improved and increased user involvement.

■ Earlier feedback from end users can be obtained by the designer.

■ The avoidance of the expense and difficulty of changing a finished software product.

The disadvantages of prototyping include:

■ End-user confusion between the prototype and finished system.

■ Excessive development time of the prototype.

This methodology should not be used where user requirements are well established or the system is a standard one used by the organisation.

Rapid application development (RAD)

The main aim of **rapid application development (RAD)** is to produce a software solution in less than six months (considered to be the longest time scale over which user requirements will stay static). RAD has two main features:

- The use of joint application design (JAD) workshops – these aim to develop a set of requirements that should not change before the system is implemented.

- The use of timeboxing – the requirements of the system are defined in small 'chunks', each of which is considered using a JAD. Each 'chunk' is allocated a timescale which must not be exceeded. At the start of each timebox the objectives are defined and, at the end of the timebox, if they are not successfully completed then they may be added to another timebox or dropped.

The benefits of RAD include:

- End users are involved at all stages with the system being implemented within six months.

- End users are involved in the evaluations so this should ensure that the final system fully meets their defined requirements.

- End users do not have to define all the requirements of the system at the beginning of the process.

The disadvantages of RAD include:

- The solution developed using RAD may, on the surface, meet the end-user requirements but the functionality may not be acceptable.

- The project manager, who is overseeing the development of the system, will need to keep a very tight control over the whole development process and the team, if the system is to be developed within the six months deadline required by RAD.

This methodology should not be used where the user requirements include safety critical components.

Exam question

1 Describe, including the advantages and disadvantages, the rapid application development (RAD) methodology.

[8 marks]

Examiner hints and tips

Think about the following in relation to the question on the left.

The question asks you to describe the RAD methodology. You should describe the main concept of RAD and then provide a description of the advantages and disadvantages. You should identify an advantage or disadvantage and then, to gain full marks, provide further descriptions.

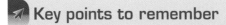

Specifications

Specification reference

3.3.1e – describe the contents of the requirements specification, the design specification and the system specification, distinguishing between them.

Keywords

Functional requirements: what the end user wants the system to do.

Non-functional requirements: the end-user defined limitations relating to response time, hardware, software and programming language.

Key points to remember

- There are three main specifications created and used during the system life cycle.
- These are the requirements, system and design specifications.

Requirements specification

This is usually developed by the systems analyst after investigations have been carried out. It is the output from the investigation and analysis stage. The contents should include:

- What the system is to do and how this is to be achieved.
- A description of all the interactions the end users will have with the software.
- The defined **functional requirements.**
- The defined **non-functional requirements.**
- The objectives/purpose of the system.
- The scope of the system.
- The proposed timescale for the project.
- End-user defined constraints including budget, time, hardware and software choices.
- A contract.

System specification

The system specification is developed from the results of the investigation of the current system and defines the requirements for the new system. The contents should include:

- The facilities and outputs that the new system will provide.
- Operation requirements – what operations the system should carry out.
- Information requirements – what information the system should provide to the end users.
- Volume requirements – for example, how much volume of processing is to be handled.
- General systems requirements, such as the degree of data accuracy needed, security issues, the need for an audit trail, the flexibility of the system and its ability to adapt to growth and change.

■ Design specification

This is usually developed by the systems designer following the investigations. The contents and focus may be slightly different depending on the type of system that is being developed. The contents should include:

- The purpose of the system.
- Assumptions, limitations or constraints.
- The inputs – documents and screens/interface.
- The outputs – documents and screens/interface.
- Error messages.
- The colours/fonts/sizes, including the consideration of the corporate image/house style to be used.
- Validation rules.
- Processing requirements/queries.
- Data structures.
- Modelling diagrams (for example, data-flow diagrams, entity-relationship diagrams and state-transition diagrams).
- The hardware.
- The software/programming language to be used.
- Test plan.

Exam question

1 Describe the contents of the system specification.   [*6 marks*]

Examiner hints and tips

Think about the following in relation to the above question.

The focus of this question is on the system specification. You should not include the contents of any other specification in your answer. You will need to identify each component of the contents and then provide further description. If you simply list the component parts of the system specification you will not achieve full marks.

1.5 Testing

Specification reference

3.3.1d – describe the purpose of test data and explain the importance of testing and test plans.

Keywords

Normal data: data that is correct and should not generate any errors on data entry.

Extreme data: data that is correct but is at the upper and/or lower boundaries of tolerance. Errors should not be generated on data entry.

Erroneous (incorrect) data: data that is incorrect and will generate errors on data entry. This data may be outside of the boundaries of tolerance or of the wrong type.

Key point to remember

■ Testing checks that a system works as it should and is free from errors before being implemented.

Testing is important and should:

■ Make sure that the system (software) meets the design specification.

■ Make sure that the system returns the correct results and actually works.

■ Give confidence to the end users – they will have more faith and confidence in a new system if it has sucessfully completed and passed all the tests.

Test data used for testing should cover:

■ **Normal data.**

■ **Extreme data.**

■ **Erroneous (incorrect) data**.

A test plan must be created before testing takes place. This lists all the tests that should be carried out. The test plan should cover:

■ The requirements.

■ Pathways.

■ Validation routines.

■ A comparison of the actual performance against the design specification.

The test plan should be in sufficient detail to enable a third party to recreate the tests and results obtained, and may be passed to the end user when the system has been installed. The standard format of a test plan is shown below:

Test no	Description of test	Type of test	Data used	Expected result

Exam question

1 Explain the importance of testing a system prior to it being installed. **[4 marks]**

Examiner hints and tips

Think about the following in relation to the question on the left.

The question requires you to explain why a system should be tested. The focus of this question is on the process of testing and its importance before a system is installed for the client.

1.6 The project team

Specification reference

3.3.1f – describe the roles and responsibilities of the following members of the project team: project manager, systems analyst, systems designer, programmer and tester.

Key points to remember

- Many people are involved in the creation of a new system.
- They may not be involved in all stages of the system life cycle.

■ The project team

Each member of the team will have different roles and responsibilities. It is possible that one person may take on more than one role.

Project manager – main role is to plan and control the whole project and is, if required, responsible for identifying and rectifying potential problems and issues.

Systems analyst – main role is to analyse and investigate the existing system. The results of the analysis will enable the systems analyst to assess the suitability of the current system for upgrading.

Systems designer – builds on the results of the findings of the systems analyst to design the new system. Their role is central to the process of designing, developing and implementing the defined requirements of the system.

Programmer – creates software that is required for the system being developed. A programmer can be a specialist in one area (language) of computer programming or a generalist who writes code for many kinds of software.

Tester – responsibilities include developing and using test plans to test the programs and modules that are included in the system. The tester must ensure that the system is free from bugs and errors.

Exam question

1 Describe the roles and responsibilities of the project manager.

[6 marks]

Examiner hints and tips

Think about the following in relation to the above question.

The focus of the question is on the roles and responsibilities of the project manager. You need to consider in your answer the interaction between the project manager and other members of the team but this is not the main focus of the question.

1.7 ERD, state transition, DFD and flowcharts

Specification reference

3.3.1h – describe, interpret and create entity relationship diagrams, state transition diagrams, data flow diagrams and flowcharts and, for each, explain its suitability for use in a given application.

Key points to remember

- During the design stage of the system life cycle different techniques can be used to complete data modelling.
- These include entity relationship diagrams, state transition diagrams, data flow diagrams and flowcharts.

Keywords

Entity relationship diagram (ERD): a diagram that represents the structure of data in a software system using entities and the relationships between those entities.

Data flow diagram (DFD): shows how data moves through a system. A DFD shows who the system interacts with in the form of external entities.

An **entity relationship diagram (ERD)** comprises:

- Entities – a 'thing' that can be uniquely identified, for example, a product.

- Attributes – the information that is held on a system about an entity, for example, for a product these could be product number, description, supplier.

- Primary key – a unique field in a table, that identifies each occurrence of an entity. Used when creating relationships.

- Foreign key – the primary key from a different table.

- Relationships – how entities are linked. There are three types of relationships – 1:1, M:1 and M:M. A M:M relationships can be decomposed using a link entity.

A **data flow diagram (DFD)**:

- Shows who/what the system interacts with in the form of external entities.

- Focuses on the processes that transform incoming data flows (inputs) into outgoing data flows (outputs).

- Shows how the processes create and use data that is held in data stores.

- Does not show the hardware or software required to operate the system.

- Shows the data stores that are used and the direction of flow of data and information.

- Has rules about how the components can be linked.

- Can be shown as a Level 0 (L0), or context diagram, giving a summary of the system.

- Can be a Level 1 (L1) providing an overview of what is happening within the system, represented in the L0 by the central process box.

A **state transition diagram (STD):**

- Defines every state of a system diagrammatically.

- Shows each state as a location, and the transitions between them as arrows. Each arrow is labelled with the reason for the state transition.

- Enables the state of a system to be followed as different stimuli arrive.

- Shows the actions (outputs) associated with each transition.

- Is formal, so tools can be built which can execute them.

- Is ideal for describing the behaviour of a single object.

- Is not good at describing behaviour that involves several objects.

A **flowchart:**

- Is good for providing a general outline of the processing that is involved in the system under investigation.

- Does not relate very well to the actual software system which is eventually developed.

- Uses different shaped symbols to represent different actions.

- Can be used to model all kinds of systems not just computer systems.

- Can be used to break a process into small steps or to give an overview of a complete system.

- Can be easily understood by people who are not involved in the IT industry.

- Does not translate easily into code.

- Can sometimes become so complex it is hard to follow.

- Is used by the analyst to give a generalised overview of a system or the functions which make up a specific process.

Exam question

1 Describe flowcharts and explain how they can be used in the system life cycle. [*8 marks*]

Examiner hints and tips

Think about the following in relation to the above question.

The focus of this question is on the use of flowcharts to model data. You should not include any other data-modelling tools in your answer. You will need to describe flowcharts and how they can be used by the systems analyst. You should include the advantages and disadvantages of using flowcharts.

1.8 CPA and Gantt charts

Specification reference

3.3.1g – describe, interpret and create critical path analysis (CPA) and Gantt charts as tools for project planning.

Key point to remember

■ A project manager can use several project planning tools to plan a project. These include critical path analysis (CPA) and Gantt charts.

Keywords

Critical path analysis (CPA): shows the relationship between the different parts of the project. The process of identifying how the tasks within a project fit together so that all tasks occur in a logical order.

Gantt charts: a diagram that shows each task as a block of time. Each block of time is labelled with the title/description of the task and the amount of time the block represents.

■ Critical path analysis (CPA)

■ Identifies the critical path for a project – the order in which the component parts have to be completed and, usually, the path that takes the maximum time.

■ Defines the path that should be taken to ensure the project is successful and completed on time.

■ Enables resources to be allocated provisionally.

■ Enables slack, lead and lag time to be built in to cover any slippage in the project.

■ Provides a firm idea of when tasks and the project should be completed.

■ Gantt charts

■ Show how long each activity/task is expected to take and the order in which these will occur.

■ Contain:

■ Milestones – important checkpoints or interim goals for a project.
■ Resources – people/equipment needed.
■ Status – shows the progress of each task.
■ Dependencies – activities which are dependent on other activities being completed first or at the same time.

■ Enable the modelling of how long the overall project will take and where the projected pressure points are.

■ Show the critical path as the longest sequence of dependent tasks.

Exam question

1 Describe how Gantt charts can be used as a tool for project planning. [*4 marks*]

Examiner hints and tips

Think about the following in relation to the question on the left.

The question requires you to describe how Gantt charts can be used when planning a project. You will need to identify features of a Gantt chart and then expand your answer to describe how they can be used.

2 Designing computer-based information systems

Processing

Specification reference

3.3.2a – discuss batch, interactive and real-time processing systems in terms of processing methods, response time and user interface requirements.

 Key point to remember

- There are many different types of processing systems. These are known as modes of operation or operational modes.

 Keywords

Batch processing system: processes batches of data at regular intervals.

Interactive processing system: handles transactions one at a time.

Real-time processing system: processes data at the time it is required.

There are three main processing systems:

- **Batch**
- **Interactive**
- **Real-time**.

These are all different in terms of processing, response time and user interface requirements. These differences are shown in the table below.

	Batch	Interactive	Real-time
Processing	Processed when the system is not busy and off-line.	Each transaction is completed before moving onto the next.	Data is processed as soon as it is received by the processor.
Response time	Delayed: there is a delay between the data being input and the results. This can be overnight or days.	Dependent on action from end user.	Very quick, based on user requirements, but usually lower than four seconds.
User interface requirements	Usually code based.	Graphical User Interface (GUI).	Usually based on the internal requirements of the user.

Exam question

1 Explain the differences in terms of response time between the processing systems.
[6 marks]

Examiner hints and tips

Think about the following in relation to the question on the left.

The question requires you to explain the differences in response time between the three processing systems. You must consider all three systems in your answer and relate your answer only to response times.

Human–computer interface (HCI)

Specification reference

3.3.2c – discuss the use of colour, layout, quantity of information on screen, size of font, complexity of language and type of controls when designing a human–computer interface.

Key point to remember

■ The designer must consider the needs of the user at all times when a human–computer interface (HCI) is being designed.

When designing a **human–computer interface (HCI)** the designer must consider the:

Keyword

White space: the amount of empty space on a screen.

Use of colour

■ The colours used should follow the corporate colours. However, care should be taken so the colours do not clash. Colours should be chosen that enable a user with a sight impediment to use the HCI.

■ Colour can be used to trigger the memory of the user.

■ The number of colours used should be limited to four per screen and seven for the whole sequence of screens.

■ Colours can be used to code information but the user must understand the code and the colours should match the users' expectations.

■ Colours can be used to attract the users' attention. The most effective colours for this are white, yellow and red.

Layout

■ All screens of the HCI should have a consistent layout, following the house style or corporate image of the business.

■ The layout should follow that of the original source documents.

■ The layout of the information given and that to be input by the user should flow in a logical order.

■ The layout should include some **white space**.

■ Information that needs attending to immediately should always be displayed in a prominent position.

■ A consistent layout will enable users to become familiar with the layout quickly, increasing confidence and learning.

Quantity of the information on the screen

■ The amount of information available should enable the users to use the screen effectively and complete the tasks.

■ Too much information on the HCI can confuse the user when they are trying to locate the required information.

Font

- The text used on the HCI must be in a font style that is easy to read.
- The font size selected needs to be appropriate to the HCI and the users.
- The font style and size of any instruction must be clear and be used consistently.

Complexity of the language

- The complexity of the language should be kept as low as possible.
- Error messages and instructions should be given in simple language.
- The language used should be helpful and simple but not perceived as condescending by the user.
- Technical language should be kept to a minimum but should be fit for purpose.

Type of controls

- Controls can be included to ensure ease of use, including: macros, buttons, forms and menus.
- A macro enables the user to automate tasks that are performed on a regular basis by using a button on the HCI.
- Buttons can be used to take the user to a specified page or to run a selected action/command.
- Forms can be used to assist in the entry of data. Help, guidance, instructions and error messages can be included on forms. Forms can also include validation. Forms may include drop-down boxes, option boxes and fill-in boxes.
- Menus enable a user to select actions. The three main types are: full-screen, pop-up and pull-down. Each type of menu gives the user choices of actions that are and are not available.

The designer must also ensure that the HCI is easy to learn and use. This will minimise the training required and the number of instructions that will need to be learned and remembered by the user.

Exam question

1 Explain how layout should be considered when designing an HCI. [6 marks]

Examiner hints and tips

Think about the following in relation to the question on the left.

The focus of this question is on the layout of an HCI and how this should be considered when an HCI is designed. You should also consider the layout and the impact the layout will have on the users of the HCI. You should not include any other considerations in your answer.

2.3

Operating systems

Specification reference

3.3.2b – describe the difference between types of operating systems (single-user, multi-user, multi-tasking, interactive, real-time, batch processing and distributed processing systems) by identifying their major characteristics.

Keyword

Operating system (OS): software that is responsible for allocating various system resources, for example, memory, processor time and peripheral devices such as printers and the monitor. All application programs will use the operating system to gain access to the system resources.

Key point to remember

■ An operating system (OS) is a program or suite of programs which controls the entire operation of the computer system.

There are many different types of **operating system (OS)** available, including:

- Single-user – provides access to the OS for one user at a time. The OS can support more than one user account but only one account can be used at any one time.

- Multi-user – more than one user can access the system at the same time. Access to this OS is usually provided by a network.

- Multi-tasking – the processor does more than one task at a time, for example, enabling a user to write a letter and use the internet at the same time.

- Interactive – provides direct user interaction whilst a program is running.

- Real-time – developed for real-time applications and typically used for embedded applications (systems within another application).

- Batch processing – processes batches of data at regular intervals. The amount of data processed is usually large with the data being of identical type.

- Distributed processing – a number of computers connected together with each computer completing part of the processing. When all the processing has been completed, the results are combined to meet the requirements of the user.

Exam question

1 Describe the differences between a multi-tasking and a multi-user operating system. [*4 marks*]

Examiner hints and tips

Think about the following in relation to the above question.

The question requires you to describe the differences between multi-user and multi-tasking operating systems. You must consider both of these systems in your answer and provide clear descriptions of the differences.

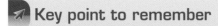

2.4 Dialogue

Specification reference

3.3.2d – discuss different methods of dialogue that allow interaction between computer and person, person and computer and computer and computer.

Keyword

Graphical user interface (GUI): a user interface based on graphics (icons, pictures and menus) instead of text; uses a mouse as well as a keyboard as an input device.

Key point to remember

- There are four main methods of dialogue that can be used to allow interaction between a computer and a person. These are prompts, nature of input, methods of input and feedback.

The designer will select the most appropriate method of dialogue depending on their investigations and the tasks and requirements. All methods of dialogue will differ between interfaces.

Prompts

Most commonly used in a command line interface and denotes that the input of an appropriate command is required from the user. Icons can be used as prompts in a **graphical user interface (GUI)** which means that the dialogue should be intuitive and simple to use.

Nature of input

Interactive interfaces will decide the nature of the next user input based on the response to the previous inputs. If forms are being used, the next responses required will be decided based on a predetermined sequence of inputs.

Methods of input

The usual method of input for a command line is a keyboard. If the interface is form-based then the user will require a keyboard and mouse. A touch screen could also be used.

Feedback

This could be in the form of menus, leading to sub-menus, to provide a large selection of choices. In a real-time or interactive interface, the feedback will provide very specific and limited choices because the responses given will limit the response given.

Exam question

1 Explain how feedback can be used as a method of dialogue between a computer and person. [*4 marks*]

Examiner hints and tips

Think about the following in relation to the question on the left.

The focus of the question is on the use of feedback between a computer and a person. You will need to concentrate only on the dialogue between a person and a computer when answering the question.

Human–device communications

Specification reference

3.3.2e – discuss the concept and implication of good methods of human–device communications, particularly human–computer interfaces (HCIs) using command line interfaces, menus/sub-menus, graphical user interfaces (GUIs), natural languages (including speech input–output) and forms dialogue.

Key point to remember

- Many devices use an embedded HCI to enable the user to complete tasks.

Devices which use an embedded HCI include mobile phones, satellite navigation systems and washing machines.

- The main, but sometimes secondary, purpose of a mobile phone is to make and receive phone calls. Many mobile phones enable users to complete other tasks. These phones will have different methods of HCI.

- A BlackBerry and an iPhone both include embedded systems to enable the user to perform some tasks. But they have different methods of communication with the user.

- A BlackBerry uses menus and sub-menus to enable the user to select the task they need to complete. The menus that are given are those that are embedded in the HCI and are not customisable by the user.

BlackBerry

- All options are available through the selection of the appropriate menus and sub-menus, for example, to make phone calls, to email, use the organiser, browse the internet and access instant messaging.

- An iPhone uses a customisable GUI as the main platform for the HCI.

- Users can rearrange the icons they see and add, or delete, their own icons on the GUI.

- The iPhone does use some menus. If a menu is being used then the back button, to move up the menu structure, is always displayed in the top left of the screen.

Apple iPhone

- Some satellite navigation (satnav) devices use a natural-language HCI. This enables a user to input, through speech, the address or postcode they wish to travel to.

- A satnav can use speech as an output to direct the driver to their destination.

- Forms can also be used to input a destination. This method of input can enable the satnav to offer the user destinations based on each element of the inputted postcode. The user is able to, based on a part input, select the destination they want.

- Forms can also be used to select options for the journey. For example, shortest distance, quickest time or different road types.

As technology develops, devices will begin to utilise different HCI methods. The designers of these devices must ensure that the HCI selected is appropriate to the tasks the users need to complete and that the advances in technology do not render the devices incapable of delivering their primary function.

TomTom GO 530

Exam question

1 Explain how a natural-language HCI can be used with a satellite navigation system.
[*6 marks*]

Examiner hints and tips

Think about the following in relation to the question on the left.

The focus of this question is on the use of a natural-language HCI and a satellite navigation system. Your answer should focus only on these requirements and should not include any other types of HCI or devices.

Perception, attention, memory and learning

Specification reference

3.3.2f – explain how a potential user's perception, attention, memory and learning can be taken into account when designing an interface.

Key point to remember

- When designing an HCI the designer will have to consider the users' perception, attention, memory and learning.

■ Perception

- A user perceives input from the sights and sounds taken from the user interface.
- Users have preconceived ideas that they draw upon when using an interface.
- For example, graphics or text in red, based on the perception of the user, mean 'stop', whilst those in green indicate 'go'.
- The use of sounds is important as users can perceive sounds as being happy (a positive response) or sad (a negative response).
- If a user hears a negative, or sad, sound then their perception is they have done something wrong. But, if they hear a positive, or happy, sound then their perception is they are using the system correctly.

■ Attention

- Most users have a limited attention span, which is also linked to the amount of time someone can look at a screen.
- The designer can increase the users' attention span by making screens uncluttered with the layout in a logical order.
- The most important information on the screen needs to be obvious and screens clearly labelled.
- If data/information has to be inserted by the user, this should also be clearly labelled.
- Pop-up messages can be used to increase the users' attention.
- Flashing graphics, sounds or pop-up messages can be used to draw the users' attention to an action on the screen. However, these should be used sparingly as too many can lead to a diminished attention span.
- Screens should have a consistent layout and colour scheme.
- Menus and sub-menus should also be consistent. These should be in the same place on the screen with the words used meaning the same for each menu and sub-menu.

- If graphics are used to denote a task, for example, a pair of scissors to denote the action 'cut', then the graphic for this action should remain constant.

■ Memory

- Many users work on the same screen on a day-to-day basis and the memory of the user 'holds' the actions required to use the interface.

- Parts of the user interface are used infrequently and the designer must ensure that these screens are also easily used.

- A consistent and uncluttered page layout can help the user hold in their short-term memory the actions required to use the interface.

- The pre-existing knowledge of the user should be considered by the designer. If the user is an existing user of the interface and is using screens that are not frequently used, then the designer must ensure that the knowledge of the user enables the use of all screens in the interface.

- Consistency between screens aids the recall of the skills and knowledge required to effectively use the interface and will increase the speed at which the user learns to use the interface.

■ Learning

- To ensure that the user can easily learn to use the interface, it must draw on the user's previous experience. This includes the use of consistent (but not distracting) screen layouts, colour and menus.

- Designers should ensure that any new interface matches, as far as possible, the current system being used.

- On-screen help in the form of pop-up messages or an easy-to-use help feature can aid users in learning how to use the interface more quickly.

- The designer should ensure that the interface can be used intuitively. The designer should focus on the perception, attention and memory of the user.

Exam question

1 Explain how the user's attention and learning should be considered when a user interface is being designed.
[6 marks]

Examiner hints and tips

Think about the following in relation to the question on the left.

The focus of this question is on the designing of an HCI and how the user's attention and learning should be considered. You should not include any other considerations in your answer.

2.7 Mental models

Specification reference

3.3.2g – describe mental models and how they can be applied to the design of a user interface.

Keyword

Mental models: an explanation in someone's thought process for how something works in the real world. The mental model of the end user must be considered when a system is being designed.

Key point to remember

■ Users of computer systems can be divided into those who have some understanding of the operation of a computer and those who have little or no understanding.

- Users who have little understanding of the operation of a computer will read and follow a set of instructions with no idea of how the tasks are being processed.

■ A **mental model** can help the user operate a computer more effectively. A mental model is based on experience as well as different types of input, such as sound and visual.

■ A mental model should cover operational functions and the generic features of the software package being used.

■ A mental model should enable the user to experience the results of an action and use this to predict the actions that may be needed in another situation.

■ A mental model enables the user to predict the performance of the computer based on their past experiences.

■ An effective user interface will consider the mental models of users.

■ The design of an interface should ensure the intention of the user is translated by the interface into the appropriate activity or action to ensure that the task is completed successfully. Conversely, the action of the computer should match the anticipated action of the user.

■ The actions of the computer should be matched through the use of audio-visual indicators with the perception of the majority of users also reflected. The designer should maintain a natural method of completing an action by the user.

Exam question

1 Describe how a mental model can be applied to the design of a user interface.
[*4 marks*]

Examiner hints and tips

Think about the following in relation to the question on the left.

The question requires you to describe how a mental model can be applied when designing a user interface. You should ensure that your answer focuses on the application of the mental model and not on describing what a mental model is.

2.8 **System and mental models**

**Specification
reference**

3.3.2h – discuss the importance
of designing a system model that
matches closely the user's mental
model.

Key point to remember

■ The designer should consider the user's mental
model when designing a system model. This is to
ensure that the final product matches the user's
requirements as closely as possible.

It is important to consider the user's mental model when designing
a system model because:

■ The user should not 'get lost' whilst using the system.

■ The system should build on the experience of the user to ensure
that previous experience is used when the user is faced with any
problems that occur. For example, the same audio cue can be used
when an error occurs or a useful error message can be provided.

■ Users will bring their own preconceptions, based on their own
mental model, to a system.

■ The confidence of users increases as they use a system model.
For example, they will recognise the use of the same graphic to
perform the same tasks in a suite of applications.

Save icon from Microsoft Word and Excel

■ The speed with which the user will learn to use the system will
be increased.

Exam question

1 Explain **two** reasons why a designer should consider the user's
mental model when designing a system model.   [4 *marks*]

Examiner hints and tips

Think about the following in relation to the above question.

The question requires you to explain two reasons why the
user's mental model should be considered by a designer. In
your answer, you should identify the two reasons and then
provide extra detail.

Model Human Processor

Specification reference

3.3.2i – describe the user interface design tool known as the Model Human Processor, developed by Card, Moran and Newell, and its application.

⚷ Key point to remember

- The Model Human Processor (MHP) attempts to portray the user of a computer system as a computer system.

🔑 Keyword

Model Human Processor (MHP): developed by Card, Moran and Newell. This concept attempts to portray the user of a computer system as a computer including memory and processors.

The **Model Human Processor (MHP)** draws an analogy between the processing and storage of a computer with the perceptual, cognitive, motor and memory activities of the computer user. This is done by a visual or audible stimulus being captured by the user with the physical attributes of the stimulus being decoded. For example, the user's attention is drawn to a box on screen. The response that is needed will then be interpreted by the user. A motor response is then initiated to satisfy the response needed, for example, the click of a mouse.

■ The application of the MHP

The model was developed to be applied to the design of a user interface. Examples of how the model can be applied to the design of a user interface include:

- The use of a logical order to the inputs, possibly those required from the user.

- An on-screen flashing cursor used to show the user where data is to be input.

- An audible stimulus, for example, a beep sound, to indicate when an error has been made by the user.

Exam question

1 Identify and explain **two** examples of how the Model Human Processor can be applied when designing a user interface.

[*4 marks*]

Examiner hints and tips

Think about the following in relation to the above question.

The question requires you to identify two examples of how the MHP can be applied during the designing of a user interface. To achieve full marks, you should provide some explanation for each of the examples you identify.

Intranet, internet and extranet

 Specification reference

3.3.3b – discuss the characteristics and purpose of intranets, the internet and extranets.

 Key points to remember

■ An extranet uses the internet to access an intranet.
■ An intranet is private and the internet is public.
■ An extranet is a private network that sits on top of the public internet.

Keyword

Internet protocol (IP): this is a protocol used for communicating data across a packet-switched internet using the internet protocol suite (TCP/IP). The IP delivers packets from the source host to the destination host based on their addresses.

An intranet is a communication system that is restricted and internal to a company or organisation – usually over a LAN or a virtual private network (VPN).

It provides an organisation with services that are only accessible by authorised users. It uses the **internet protocol (IP)** and includes access to web pages, email and collaborative working.

The internet is a global system of interconnected computer networks that use the IP. It provides access to information and resources from any connected computer anywhere in the world. It includes access to libraries, academic works, as well as internet email, chatting, on line purchasing, etc. Its purpose is to link computers and information together.

An extranet is a private network that is built on top of, and uses the internet. It is commonly used to access a company or organisation's intranet – it is easiest if thought of as an intranet accessed from any computer connected to the internet.

Weblink

http://www.zakon.org/robert/internet/timeline/

Hobbes' internet timeline.

Exam questions

1 Describe how a company could make use of an intranet.
[4 marks]

2 Describe the characteristics of the internet. [4 marks]

Examiner hints and tips

Think about the following in relation to the questions on the left.

Question 1: This question is focusing on the purpose of an intranet and how the company can make use of it. Remember, identify and then exemplify/give an example to be awarded the second mark for each point.

Question 2: Identify and exemplify two characteristics. The obvious ones to choose from are: IP, remote access and the internet's resources.

3.2 Networks

Specification reference

3.3.3a – compare the characteristics of a local area network (LAN), a wide area network (WAN) and a virtual network.

Weblink

http://computer.howstuffworks.com/vpn.htm

How virtual private networks work.

⬈ Key points to remember

■ You need to know the characteristics of each in order to compare them.

■ A virtual network is also known as a virtual private network (VPN) and requires a network underpinning it in order to work.

A LAN is a set of computers that are:

▪ Within a locally defined area and in close proximity to each other.

▪ Able to have direct connections between them.

▪ Connected only by cables that are owned by the user.

▪ Able to share local peripherals.

A LAN is usually a small **network** – often within a school, library, doctor's surgery or small business.

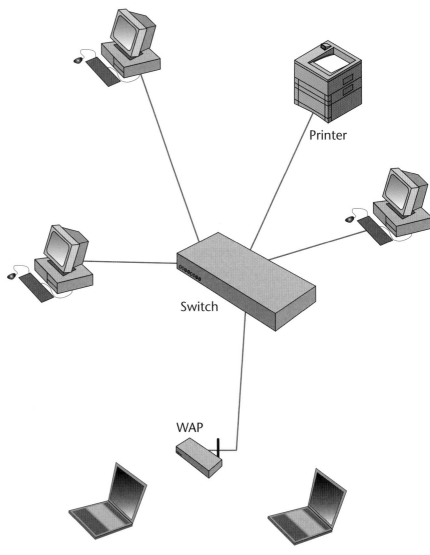

Printer

Switch

WAP

A LAN configuration

A WAN is a set of computers that are:

- Geographically remote – with large distances between them.
- Connected by equipment that is owned by a third party – telecommunications lines, satellites, etc.

The most common example of a WAN is the internet.

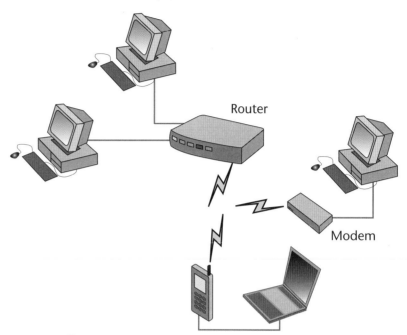

A WAN configuration

A virtual network is a network that is run on top of a larger network – it is a subset. The virtual network is then secured and acts as a private network. The computers can be physically remote but act as though they are on a local network and access local resources.

Exam questions

1 Compare the characteristics of a LAN and a WAN.   [3 marks]

2 Describe the characteristics of a virtual network.   [4 marks]

Examiner hints and tips

Think about the following in relation to the above questions.

Question 1: Identify three characteristics that are common to both – location, speed and cables – and describe how the characteristics apply to the different networks.

Question 2: You need to identify the characteristics that are applicable to a virtual network and exemplify. Make sure that you do not give the characteristics of physical networks.

3.3

Client–server and peer-to-peer

Specification reference

3.3.3c – describe client–server and peer-to-peer networks giving advantages and disadvantages of each.

 Keyword

Client: a computer/node that accesses services and data from another source, usually a server.

Weblink

http://www.techsoup.org/ learningcenter/networks/ page4772.cfm

Peer-to-peer networks.

Key points to remember

- Both peer-to-peer and client–server are types of network whose function is to allow the sharing of data/resources.
- The advantages of one tend to be the disadvantages of the other.

Peer-to-peer

In a peer-to-peer network, all the computers connected to it are of equal status. An example would be linking two home computers together. Any of the computers connected can provide printer or file-sharing resources.

Advantages	Disadvantages
Only normal computers are required – there is no need to purchase an expensive server.	Each computer is fulfilling more than one role – it may be printing or file sharing. This increases the load.
Each user manages their own computer. This means that a network manager is not required.	Data can be stored on any computer – there is no organisation to data storage.
Set-up is done via wizards within software. No technical knowledge is required.	Security, anti-virus and backup are down to the individual user.
There is no reliance on a central computer – less to go wrong.	

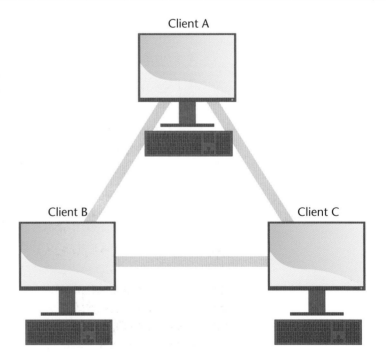

Peer-to-peer network with three computers

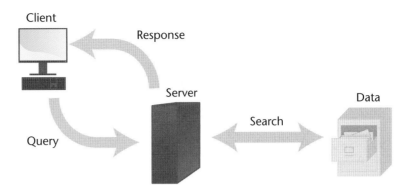

Keyword

Server: a computer that provides services to other computer clients. These services can include file storage, security and application delivery amongst others.

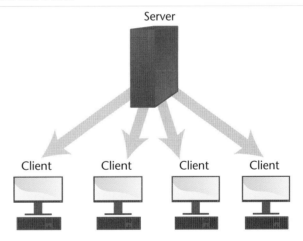

Weblink

http://www.techsoup.org/ learningcenter/networks/ page4773.cfm

Setting up a client–server network.

■ Client–server

A client–server network has a powerful controlling computer – the server. This computer controls the peripherals – printers, backup, etc., and the security of the network.

Advantages	Disadvantages
Backup, security and anti-virus are centralised.	The server costs money, as does the network operating system.
The user does not do any of the management of the computers, there is usually a network manager to do this.	A network manager is required and this costs money.
Network processing is done centrally, not at individual computers, freeing them to do what the user wants.	There is a reliance on the central server – if it fails, no work can be done.

Client-server network

Exam questions

1 Describe **two** advantages of installing and using a peer-to-peer network. [*4 marks*]

2 Describe what is meant by a client–server network. [*4 marks*]

Examiner hints and tips

Think about the following in relation to the questions on the left.

Question 1: Make sure the advantages are different and clear. They should, in the examination, relate to the context of the exam paper.

Question 2: This is a straight definition. You should identify and exemplify two points about a client–server network. You can, if you think it will help, draw a labelled diagram.

Network components

Specification reference

3.3.3e – compare the role of the following network components: switches, hubs, wireless access points, network interface cards, wireless network interface cards, routers, repeaters, bridges and servers (file, applications, mail, proxy, print, backup) and identify where their use would be appropriate.

Keyword

Network component: an item of hardware that can be used to allow a computer to communicate and become part of a network.

Weblink

http://www.hardware.com/

Networking hardware.

Hub

Key points to remember

- Many of the components have functions which duplicate each other.
- You need to be able to describe them and know where and how they should be used.

Network components

Switch – a switch has a number of ports and it stores the addresses of all devices that are directly or indirectly connected to each port. As data comes into the switch, it is examined to see the final destination and then directed to the port to which the device it is seeking is connected.

Hub – this is a concentrator that connects lots of computers to the network through a single link. Signals received on any port are broadcast to all other ports. Hubs can be active (where they repeat signals sent through them) or passive (where they do not repeat but merely split signals sent through them).

Network interface card (NIC) – this allows the device to be physically connected to the network and allows communication to pass to and from a computer. It contains a unique identifier or MAC code.

A Wireless Network Interface Card would perform the same function but eliminate the need for a direct physical connection. It can be internal or external.

Wireless access point (WAP) – if you have any wireless NICs, then you need a device that will send and receive wireless signals. A WAP is connected into the physical network by a cable and positioned so that it can send and receive wireless signals.

Router – this is a device that routes information between networks. It can select the best path to route a message, as well as translate information from one network to another. It can connect a LAN to a WAN.

Repeater – this is used in a network to strengthen a signal as it is passed along the network cable. A signal degrades over distance so a repeater can boost the signal and extend the maximum cable length.

Bridge – a bridge connects and passes packets between two network segments that use the same communications protocol. This allows data to be broadcast in one direction rather than broadcast in many.

Server – there are several different kinds of server:

- **File server:** stores documents and resources and allows access to those by computer and user.

Rack-mounted servers

- **Proxy server:** verifies and routes requests and bans those that are not permitted.

- **Applications server:** stores and distributes programs to users, keeps quotas of instances of applications running to ensure licence agreements are not broken.

- **Email server:** routes email as well as holds email and email accounts.

- **Print server:** controls printing, including quotas.

- **Backup server:** stores copies of user information and files, security permissions, emails and even programs.

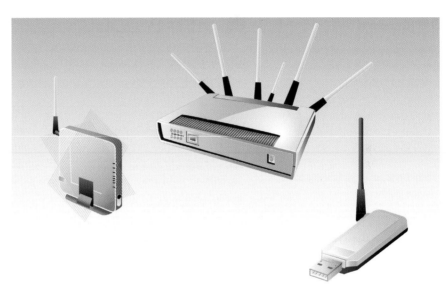

Different types of wireless device

Exam questions

1 Compare the use of a hub and a switch in a network. [*3 marks*]

2 Describe, giving examples of use, **two** different servers that could be used in a network. [*4 marks*]

Examiner hints and tips

Think about the following in relation to the above questions.

Question 1: The hub and switch have similar functions but there are also some differences. Identify three features to compare and show how these features apply to hubs and switches.

Question 2: The choice of servers is yours. Identify, describe their functions and give an example of how each would be used.

Optical communication

Specification reference

3.3.3f – describe optical communication methods (infrared, fibre optic, laser), their advantages and disadvantages and typical applications.

Key points to remember

- This only covers fibre optics, laser and infrared.
- Fibre-optic signals use light but run within a cable (glass/plastic fibre).
- Optical communications use light as a carrier of information (as opposed to electrical signals).

> ### Keyword
>
> **Fibre optic:** a glass fibre that carries light. The fibres can be wrapped in bundles.

Weblinks

http://jvsc.jst.go.jp/live/kagaku_e/index_e.htm

How optical communications work.

http://www.arcelect.com/fibercable.htm

Fibre optics.

Fibre optic

Fibre-optic cables are capable of conducting modulated light transmission.

Advantages	Disadvantages
High bit rate – handles both speech and data.	More expensive than other networking media.
Better quality service as it is less susceptible to interference.	Only economical when the bandwidth is fully utilised or likely to be in near future.
Unaffected by electro magnetic disturbance (voltages, clicks, atmosphere).	High cost of installation compared with copper wires.
Difficult to tap into them – secure.	
Large distances covered.	

Light amplification by stimulated emission of radiation (laser)

A laser outputs a focused electromagnetic energy field in which all waves are at the same frequency and aligned in phase.

Advantages	Disadvantages
Data transferred at high speeds.	Line of sight required (signal can be bounced).
Used in locations where laying cable is not an option.	Can be blocked by fog/mist.

Fibre-optic cables

Infrared

Infrared is a focused ray of light in the infrared frequency spectrum. It is measured in terahertz, or trillions of hertz (cycles per second), modulated with information and sent from a transmitter to a receiver over a relatively short distance.

Advantages	Disadvantages
Speed up to 4 Mb/s.	Distance between the two terminals has to be low.
No cabling.	A line of sight is always needed.
Unlicensed.	Susceptible to interference from other light sources.

Weblink

http://compnetworking.about.
com/od/homenetworking/g/bldef_
infrared.htm

Infrared.

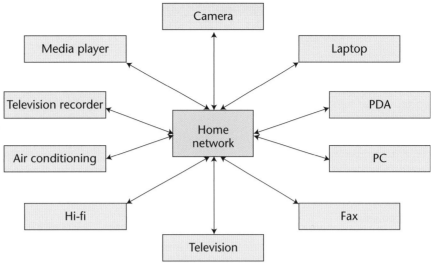

Applications of infrared

Uses

All forms of optical communications are used in high voltage installations.

Applications of infrared include mice and keyboards, car locks, printers, headphones, home security and home control systems.

Applications of fibre optics include long distance communications, lighting, signage and aircraft communications.

Applications of lasers include mapping the ocean floor and data transmission.

Exam questions

1 Describe **two** disadvantages of fibre-optic communication.
[*4 marks*]

2 Describe how an organisation could make use of infrared communication. [*4 marks*]

Examiner hints and tips

Think about the following in relation to the above questions.

Question 1: This is looking for two identifications and exemplifications of reasons why fibre optic should not be used.

Question 2: This is contextualised and your answer should include descriptions of two applications within an organisation. You will not get marks for saying 'to communicate'. The examples need to be specific and relevant.

3.6 **Bandwidth**

Specification reference

3.3.3d – explain the importance of bandwidth when transmitting data and how different types of communication media (cables, wireless, optical) govern the bandwidth available.

Keyword

Communication media: the physical means used to transfer data – typically cable but can also include optical methods and satellite.

Weblink

http://www.bandwidthplace.com/

Test your bandwidth.

Key points to remember

- Bandwidth is NOT speed, it is volume of data over time.
- Data is transferred through communications media.

Bandwidth

Bandwidth is the maximum amount of data that can travel over a given data transmission channel in a given amount of time. The more bandwidth you have, the more data you can move in the same amount of time. Bandwidth is only important when talking about time-sensitive data. Video that is downloaded and watched off-line does not need a large bandwidth. Video streaming, where it is being watched in real time, needs a high bandwidth so that there is no jerkiness of the picture and the sound is synched.

Communication media

The media used to carry the signal will have an effect on the bandwidth that is available.

Wireless signal strength (and therefore bandwidth) is based on distance between sender/receiver and stability (obstructions between sender and receiver).

Copper cable has distance limitations and is subject to electrical interference, both of which reduce bandwidth.

Fibre-optic cable enables longer distance than copper and is not subject to electrical interference.

Exam questions

1 Describe the importance of bandwidth when streaming a concert.
[4 marks]

2 Describe factors that govern bandwidth in wireless communication.
[4 marks]

Examiner hints and tips

Think about the following in relation to the questions on the left.

Question 1: This is not asking for a definition of bandwidth but its relevance to streaming video.

Question 2: You need to identify two factors and then for each, describe how they govern bandwidth.

3.7 Wireless communication

Specification reference

3.3.3g – describe wireless communication methods (Bluetooth®, radio), their advantages, disadvantages and typical applications.

Keywords

Bluetooth®: a protocol for connecting headset to phone or connecting computer to mobile Personal Data Assistant (PDA).

Wireless: for creating a network, for example, sharing an internet connection at home. Connecting mobile phone/PDA to Wi-Fi networks (The Cloud, for example).

Weblink

http://www.bluetooth.com/ bluetooth/

The official Bluetooth® site.

Key points to remember

■ Bluetooth® uses radio technology and has many of the same advantages and disadvantages as Wi-Fi.

■ Wireless communication is the transfer of information without the use of electrical conductors (wires).

Bluetooth®

This is a protocol that has become synonymous with a method of communication. **Bluetooth®** has a range of approximately 10m.

Advantages	Disadvantages
Communication between the two devices can be made secure with a key.	There is a limit on both the data transfer rate and the distance between the devices.
It can work without a line of sight between the devices.	It allows connectivity to only one device at a time.
Many portable devices now make use of the technology.	

Radio

Wireless or Wi-Fi networks also use radio technology.

Advantages	Disadvantages
Does not require physical connection between devices – this allows for no line of sight and physical obstructions between devices.	Signal strength can be reduced by distance and obstacles.
A worldwide standard exists allowing many devices to connect.	Can have security vulnerabilities (if not correctly set up).
	Bandwidth linked to number of connected devices.

Exam questions

1 Describe **two** advantages to a homeowner of using wireless in their home. [4 marks]

2 Describe **two** ways that a warehouse could make use of Bluetooth®. [4 marks]

Examiner hints and tips

Think about the following in relation to the questions on the left.

Question 1: This is related specifically to the advantages of wireless for home use. Answers can focus on lack of wires and disruption and shared connectivity.

Question 2: The answer needs to be contextualised to a warehouse.

3.8

Communication applications

Specification reference

3.3.3h – describe the facilities of the following communication applications: fax, email, bulletin (discussion) boards, tele/videoconferencing and internet relay chat (IRC) and compare their use for a given application.

Key points to remember

- Facilities are things the application can do.
- You need to be able to describe facilities and compare applications.

> **Keyword**
>
> **Communications:** transmitting information from one person to another – via text, sound or images.

Weblink

http://communication. howstuffworks.com/email.htm

How email works.

Fax

Advantages	Disadvantages
If the sending and the receiving equipment is compatible then faxes can be sent and received in colour, otherwise they are received in black and white.	The received document cannot be directly edited.
A fax machine gives a receipt of delivery to the number you entered.	There is no guarantee of where you are sending the fax to and who may see it.
Modern fax machines have the ability to hold address books and to send faxes to groups of people.	The quality is variable – it depends on the quality of the sending and receiving machines and the original.

Email

- Email allows you to send messages to many people at the same time – using lists of people and by sending carbon copies.
- It is possible to add a digital signature to the message and encrypt the message to increase security.
- The email client can send back a confirmation of delivery and of opening, but with some software it is possible to cancel this and stop it from being sent.
- Pictures and text can be sent and, providing there is the correct software on the receiving computer, they can be edited.
- A single point of contact (email address) can be picked up anywhere in the world.
- An email can sit on a server until the recipient is ready to read it, improving security.
- Facilities also include distribution lists and address books.

Internet relay chat (IRC)

IRC is real-time messaging with groups of people or individuals. It is a text version of teleconferencing. In some versions, pictures can be sent and the conversation can be recorded.

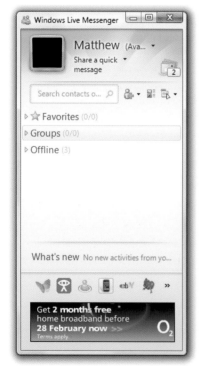

Example of IRC

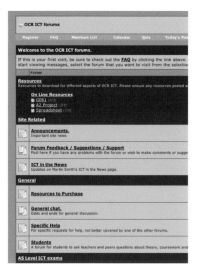

Example of a bulletin board

Bulletin boards

- A bulletin board is a website where users can post and read messages from other users.

- A bulletin board can be accessed through the internet and can be used to give information or contain links to downloadable documents.

- A bulletin board is accessible anywhere in the world and can have many recipients.

- Parts of a bulletin board can be password protected as can the documents that are downloaded. Parts of a bulletin board can also be set aside for selected groups of users.

- A bulletin board can set up threads of conversations and ensure that all posts are kept together. Users can be notified by email of new postings.

- Bulletin boards can have posts moderated before they are made accessible to users.

Tele/videoconferencing

Teleconferencing and videoconferencing enable communication to take place between groups of people who are geographically remote. Teleconferencing enables participants to talk and videoconferencing includes video as well as sound.

Advantages	Disadvantages
The equipment required can be very simple and cheap (a web camera).	The equipment required can be complex and therefore very expensive.
Videoconferencing can be done via a direct line or across the internet.	Individuals involved in the conference need to be present at the same time and there can be a slight time delay that makes conversation difficult.
The conference can be recorded for playback at a later date.	Image size is usually small and the quality may be poor, especially when simple equipment is used.

Exam questions

1 Compare the use of IRC and teleconferencing for discussing sales contracts with four different people in three different continents.   [3 marks]

2 Using examples, describe **two** facilities of email.   [4 marks]

Examiner hints and tips

Think about the following in relation to the questions on the left.

Question 1: There are lots of similarities between IRC and teleconferencing as well as differences – identify three and relate IRC and teleconferencing to them.

Question 2: You need to focus on the facilities, not the use or the purpose.

3.9

Broadband

Specification reference

3.3.3i – compare different types of broadband connection and give suitable situations where the use of each would be appropriate: asymmetric digital subscriber line (ADSL), cable, wireless, leased line, satellite.

Key points to remember

- Speeds mentioned are likely to change – you need to keep up to date.
- Satellite and wireless can be mobile.

Weblink

http://www.ofcom.org.uk/media/
features/broadbandspeedsjy

OFCOM review of broadband speeds.

Asymmetric digital subscriber line (ADSL)

ADSL runs on copper cables and the frequencies that are not used for voice telephone calls. It is always on and allows the telephone to be used for speech and for data traffic at the same time.

It is used for short distances – typically 4 km. Asymmetric means that the data flow is different in one direction to the other. Usually, the download bandwidth is higher than the upload bandwidth.

Advantages	Disadvantages
High speed connection.	Service not available everywhere.
Use of the phone line while connected.	Distance from exchange limited.
No extra wiring; ADSL uses the existing phone line.	Bandwidth is not guaranteed.
	Faster download than upload.
	Typical contention ratio of 50:1 (50 users sharing bandwidth).

Wireless router

Cable

This is the use of fibre-optic cables, usually provided by television companies, to deliver an internet connection. The service is, like ADSL, asymmetric giving higher download bandwidth. Bandwidth up to 50 MB is available.

Advantages	Disadvantages
High speed connection.	Physical cable needs to be installed.
Telephone, television and internet in a single service.	Speeds advertised are not guaranteed.
Single point of contact for problems.	Limited competition.
Based on fibre optics – more reliable, consistent and secure.	Contention ratio issue where users share link.

This wireless dongle can be used to connect a computer to the internet via a mobile telephone network

Wireless

This is the use of 2G or 3G technology on mobile telephone networks to allow internet access. The mobile phone or wireless device can be tethered to a laptop to use the wireless connection. Bandwidth is limited by the contract. There are also limits to data usage.

Advantages	Disadvantages
■ Connection is not limited to home location.	■ Coverage depends on location.
■ Can connect phone or computer.	■ Limited bandwidth and possible data usage limits.
■ Technology constantly improving.	■ Expensive for the service.

Weblink

http://www.top10-broadband.co.uk/compare/wireless_mobile_broadband/

Wireless broadband packages.

🔑 **Keyword**

Broadband: a fast, permanent connection across a wide band of frequencies.

Leased line

This is a symmetric line connecting two locations. It is a direct connection that can have a high bandwidth.

Advantages	Disadvantages
■ Bandwidth is guaranteed.	■ Requires line to be installed.
■ No contention.	■ Cost of the line is high.
■ Symmetric.	

Satellite transmission

Satellite

One-way satellite **broadband** uses a satellite for downloading and a telephone line for uploading. Two-way satellite broadband uses a satellite for both uploading and downloading. Satellite broadband is often used by news companies to transmit stories for television.

Advantages	Disadvantages
■ No need for fixed lines.	■ Latency delay.
■ Can be mobile.	■ Cost of technology.
	■ Limited bandwidth.

Exam questions

1 Compare ADSL and leased line broadband connections. [*3 marks*]

2 Describe **two** ways a television company could use satellite broadband. [*4 marks*]

Examiner hints and tips

Think about the following in relation to the questions on the left.

Question 1: This is a comparison – there is no need for technicalities, general comparisons are acceptable.

Question 2: This is contextualised – be specific to how the television company could use it.

Mobile phones

Specification reference

3.3.3j – describe how a mobile phone network operates (cellular and satellite) and the advantages and disadvantages of cellular and satellite mobile phone systems and their use.

Keywords

International mobile equipment identity (IMEI): a unique identifier for every mobile device that can be used to track and even remove a phone from a network.

Public switched telephone network (PSTN): the standard telephone network.

Weblink

http://www.bizhelp24.com/it/mobile-phones-in-business-disadvantages.html

Disadvantages of mobile phones.

Key points to remember

- How satellite and cellular phones work.
- The topic covers advantages and disadvantages of use – although similar, there are specific differences.

■ Cellular network (simplified)

A mobile phone places a call by sending a 'call initiation' request to its nearest base station. This contains a unique identifier – the **nternational mobile equipment identity (IMEI)**. The base station sends the request, which contains the telephone number dialled and the IMEI, to the mobile switching centre (MSC).

The MSC validates the request:

- Is there enough credit?
- Can the user make the call (no call bar)?

and if allowed, makes a connection to the number called via the **public switched telephone network (PSTN)**.

The steps that take place when a mobile station receives an incoming call are as follows. The mobile phone, when switched on, informs the MSC that it is active within its area and continually scans for paging signals from the base station it is connected to. When a MSC receives a request for a connection to a mobile phone in its area, it sends a broadcast message to all base stations under its control. The message contains the number of the mobile station that is being called. The base station then broadcasts the message. The phone acknowledges the message. The MSC receives the acknowledgment via the base station, and instructs the base station and phone to switch to an unused channel.

Advantages	Disadvantages
■ Coverage is almost complete and phones can be used anywhere.	■ Loss of signal, battery and credit.
■ People reassured as rarely out of contact.	■ Phone can be tracked.
■ The use of the data network means pictures and text messages can be sent and web access is available.	■ Use of phones in public places can be annoying.
■ Smart phones are mini computers which can connect anywhere and anytime.	■ Phones can also distract – for example, when driving.

Satellite phone

Satellite network (simplified)

A satellite phone connects with satellites that are within its line of sight. The satellite relays the signal to another satellite or to a base station and then from the base station through the telephone network.

Depending on the type of phone you have, calls from one satellite phone to another will work in one of two ways:

- Satellite phone A to satellite, then to base station. Base station to satellite and down to satellite phone B, or

- Satellite phone A to satellite and direct to satellite phone B.

There are two types of satellites used – low earth orbit (LEO) and geosynchronous earth orbit (GEO). LEO satellites orbit between 200 and 500 miles high. They can circle the earth in 90 minutes and ensure coverage through a large number of satellites. GEO are in a fixed position above the earth. They rotate around the earth at the same speed as the earth rotates around its axis, in effect remaining stationary above a fixed point on the earth.

Advantages	Disadvantages
Can be used anywhere on the surface of the planet where there is sight of a satellite.	There needs to be line of sight with a satellite.
When the normal phone system is down the satellite phone will still work.	Solar flares and buildings can reduce the quality of connection.
Phones are getting smaller and more portable.	Bandwidth is low and cost is high compared with cellular.
There is greater security as it is harder to monitor calls.	

Exam questions

1 Identify the steps required for a call from a cellular mobile phone to be made to a landline in the same country.   [*6 marks*]

2 Describe the disadvantages of using a satellite mobile phone.   [*4 marks*]

Examiner hints and tips

Think about the following in relation to the questions on the left.

Question 1: Your answer should be a step-by-step list of the stages of making a phone call. It is a learnt response requiring six steps – one per mark.

Question 2: Outline in detail two disadvantages of using a satellite mobile phone.

3.11

Satellites

Specification reference

3.3.3k – describe how satellite communications systems are used and work in global positioning, weather, data transfer systems and television, explaining the advantages and disadvantages of using satellites for these applications.

Weblink

http://www.metoffice.gov.uk/satpics/latest_uk_ir.html

Met Office satellite images.

⚐ Key points to remember

- Satnav is not GPS, it is a system that makes use of GPS.
- There is a difference between the method the satellite uses to communicate and the use of the satellite.

▇ Global positioning system (GPS)

GPS is used to locate the users position on the ground. GPS is often combined with software – such as satnav – to plot routes from your current location to an end location. GPS is used in the construction industry for surveying as well as by the military and delivery companies.

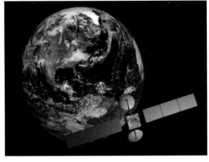

Satellite orbiting Earth

Advantages	Disadvantages
▪ High degree of accuracy.	▪ Need line of sight to satellite.
▪ Can be linked to many different applications – Satnav, Google Maps, etc.	▪ Quality dependent on the software installed not, the GPS.
	▪ Dependent on technology/batteries.

▇ Weather

These are systems that observe – they can take pictures that are sent back to earth and used to analyse weather systems. The pictures can vary – they can be 'normal photographs' or thermal/infrared. The pictures are used to monitor and predict weather patterns and look at the effects of pollution and natural disasters.

Satellite weather map

Advantages	Disadvantages
▪ The impact of natural and man-made disasters can be viewed.	▪ The images taken need to be interpreted.
▪ With geostationary satellites, the same view can be taken repeatedly.	▪ Only a certain number of photos a day can be received with a polar orbit.
▪ Weather predictions can be made and hurricane/storm warnings given.	▪ A polar orbit shows a small area in detail. A geostationary orbit shows a large area but in less detail.

Keyword

Satellite: man-made equipment that orbits the earth – either geostationary (located above a fixed point) or polar orbit (passing the same spot at the same time each day).

Weblinks

http://www.freesat.co.uk/

Freesat service.

http://www.sky.com/

Sky Service.

Satellite television receiver

Data transfer systems

Satellite systems can be used to transfer data for the internet and for other applications. All the systems covered in this section use satellites to transfer data. In addition, the banking system is a major user of satellites for transferring transaction information.

Advantages	Disadvantages
▪ Secure connection.	▪ Very high initial set-up costs.
▪ Does not need complex infrastructure to support communication.	▪ Reliant on technology working.
	▪ Requires relay satellites to cover vast distances.

Television

Satellite television is a method of giving the end user more channels than are currently available through the traditional radio waves. The system needs a decoder – usually a set-top box, and this separates the free to air channels from the encoded ones.

Advantages	Disadvantages
▪ Contains more channels than broadcast radio waves.	▪ High initial set-up cost.
▪ Remote areas that have problems receiving radio waves can receive satellite.	▪ Reliant on equipment working.
▪ Free and encrypted channels can be broadcast enabling companies to charge for services.	▪ Can be affected by weather conditions.

Exam questions

1 Describe how satellites are used to assist in weather prediction. [4 marks]

2 Describe **two** advantages of using satellites for data transfer. [4 marks]

Examiner hints and tips

Think about the following in relation to the questions on the left.

Question 1: This is a straight forward 'how' question – describe two ways that satellites can be used in weather prediction – a learnt response.

Question 2: The type of data is not specific – so you can contextualise and decide on the example yourself.

Mobile technology

3.3.3l – discuss the implications of being able to communicate from anywhere in the world using mobile technology.

Keyword

Mobile technology: devices which are portable and allow you to communicate. This requires a device to communicate (phone/webcam, etc.) and a device to make the connection.

Weblink

http://resource.findmespot.com/ spotus/videos/alaska_survivor/ video_player.swf

Using mobile technology to save lives.

Key points to remember

- In the exam the implications will be context sensitive – you need to look at the scenario in the question before formulating your answer.
- There are social, technological and financial implications.

With a combination of satellite and cellular mobile phones, it is possible to connect to the communications network from just about anywhere on the surface of the planet.

There are several positive implications. It is possible to call for help – if you are in trouble or need assistance. You can call to reassure friends and relatives of your location and situation. As a business person you can connect with your work location and gain access to emails and up-to-date information (as required by the company).

There are some disadvantages – the cost of communication can be high – both in terms of the hardware and the cost of calls. There is a need for power (although solar devices such as Powermonkey do exist) and there can be a false sense of security with a reliance on the technology (which can fail). It is also not possible to truly escape from work – there is always the possibility of being able to be contacted.

Mobile technology can also be used to connect a PDA/laptop to the internet. This gives access to social networking sites, emails and up-to-date news and weather.

SPOT GPS messenger

Exam questions

1 Describe the advantages and disadvantages of taking a satellite phone on a desert trek.   [*6 marks*]

2 Describe the disadvantages of always being able to be contacted by the office.   [*4 marks*]

Examiner hints and tips

Think about the following in relation to the questions on the left.

Question 1: The question is about satellite phones and their use in the desert. Make sure you contextualise your answer.

Question 2: This question is looking for reasons why it is not always a good thing to be in contact – for example, work interfering with personal life and holidays, and diminished responsibility as you can always contact the office for validation.

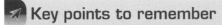

3.13 Standards and protocols

Specification reference

3.3.3m – explain the importance of standards for communicating between devices and explain how protocols are used to enable this communication.

 **Keyword**

Standard: agreed set of rules that is followed by all parties.

Weblink

http://www3.rad.com/ networks/1998/pop/index.htm

Game on the POP protocol.

Key points to remember

- A protocol is the method of implementing a standard.
- You do not need to know the specifics of any protocol or give specific examples.

A network is two or more computers connected together so that they can communicate. Without communication between the computers and the peripherals they cannot exchange information.

In order for the computers to communicate they need to be talking the same language. This means that they need to be running the same protocol. Internet protocol (IP) is one example of a protocol – this is used for devices to communicate on the internet.

A protocol is a set of communication rules. The protocol is the method by which the **standard** is implemented. Typically, a standard governs:

- The format of the message.
- The type of error checking to be used.
- Any compression.
- How the sending device indicates it has finished sending.
- How the receiving device indicates that it has received the message.

Exam questions

1 Why are standards required? [3 *marks*]

2 Describe **two** ways a protocol enables devices to communicate. [4 *marks*]

Examiner hints and tips

Think about the following in relation to the above questions.

Question 1: This is not a question about protocols but the level above – it requires more than 'to allow devices to communicate'.

Question 2: This is two features of a protocol that enable devices to communicate.

4.1 Use of telecommunications

Specification reference

3.3.4a – describe the use of telecommunication and information technology in telephone systems, banking, production control, global positioning systems, navigation and weather forecasting.

Weblink

http://www.vidly.net/collection-how-its-made.html

Production control – how it is made.

⤤ Key points to remember

■ This is not how the systems work but how they are used.

■ These are the only systems that you need to have knowledge of.

◼ Telephone systems

ICT is used in telephone systems in a number of ways. It is used in voice recognition (buying cinema tickets, for example), menu options (either voice or keypad), voicemail systems (leaving, retrieving and setting options) and ring back systems. The telephone system can allow numbers to be blocked or shown, last caller to be found out and even allow multiple calls at the same time.

It is important that your answers focus on the telephone system and not the features of the telephone.

◼ Banking

Banking services – paying money in (either manually or electronically), taking money out (via an ATM, cheque or electronically), paying bills and providing statements – can all be done in a number of ways using ICT. Banks provide these services through telephone, ATMs, internet or a terminal at the branch (in person).

Online banking

Car-building robots

Weather station

■ Production control

The manufacturing industry makes extensive use of ICT. A typical manufacturing process will involve many different stages. The machinery used to manufacture the product is often controlled by a computer, for example, robots building cars or a computer controlling the mixture or shape of a product.

ICT and production control are linked to Computer Aided Design (CAD) and Computer Aided Manufacture (CAM).

■ Global positioning systems and navigation

Global positioning systems (GPS) are used to locate a position on the surface of the Earth. Having located the position this can then be used within satnav systems to direct drivers and walkers to a new location. This can be in the form of a map and/or written/verbal directions.

GPS is used for map making and land surveying. It can also be used to identify archaeological finds and in **geocaching**.

■ Weather forecasting

This involves the use of GPS, satellite imaging and measuring devices as well as specialist modelling software.

Satellite imaging can be used to show cloud formations. Measuring devices can record a wealth of weather information and send it to a central collection station. This can then be used by computer systems for weather forecasting.

Exam questions

1 Describe how ICT can be used in the banking industry.
[*4 marks*]

2 Describe how ICT can be used in weather forecasting. [*4 marks*]

Examiner hints and tips

Think about the following in relation to the above questions.

Question 1: This is a learnt response – identify and exemplify two different ways ICT can be used by a bank.

Question 2: Again, a learnt response using the same technique as question 1, but this time applied to weather forecasting.

Television weather forecast

Software-based training methods

 Specification reference

3.3.4b – discuss the use of software-based training methods.

 Keyword

Software-based training: any computer program, whether local or delivered through the internet, that can assist the end user in learning something. Can include tests, checkpoints and revision.

Weblink

http://it.toolbox.com/blogs/enterprise-solutions/pros-and-cons-of-training-methods-16921

Advantages and disadvantages of different training methods.

Key points to remember

- This section is about the use of the methods.
- Software-based training can include online tutorials, simulated training and tests and targets.

With any system there are advantages and disadvantages to both the end user and to the trainer. Those listed below are generic and need to be contextualised and applied to the given system.

■ End user

Advantages	Disadvantages
■ The pace can be decided by the user.	■ Invasion of privacy/pressure to go faster through the material.
■ The user can redo sections that are unclear.	■ Health issues regarding computer use.
■ Different methods of learning are used – video/sound/images.	■ Requires motivation to sit and learn.
■ Feedback can be given and new targets set.	■ Needs a basic level of ICT skills.
■ Automatic feedback – no need to wait.	■ No personal intervention by a tutor.
■ Can be completed at home resulting in less pressure.	■ Completion of training does not necessarily mean anything has been learnt.

■ Trainer

Advantages	Disadvantages
■ Progress reports on students.	■ Materials may not be appropriate.
■ Can see weaknesses and strengths of students.	■ Needs to be available when the learner is using the system – may be out of hours.
■ Leaves free time to target weak students.	■ Needs to know and understand the delivery system.

Examiner hints and tips

Think about the following in relation to the questions on the left.

Question 1: There are two constraints – advantages and end user.

Question 2: Identify and exemplify, making sure to give two disadvantages.

Exam questions

1 Describe the advantages of software-based training to the end user.
   [*4 marks*]

2 Describe the disadvantages of software-based training to the trainer. [*4 marks*]

4.3 Use of networks

Specification reference

3.3.4d – discuss the use of networks of computers at work and at home.

Keyword

Network: one or more computers connected together, either physically or wirelessly in order to communicate and share data.

Weblink

http://www.microsoft.com/athome/moredone/wirelesssetup.mspx

Setting up a home wireless network.

Key points to remember

■ This section is about the use of the network, not the setting up.
■ Work and home can mix with teleworking.

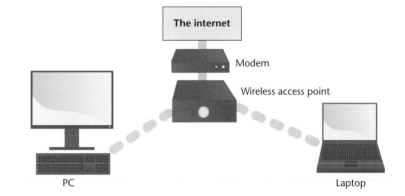

The basic function of networks, applicable to both work and home, is the communication of information. This can be through email, photographs, or documents/presentations that are being worked on.

Both work and home have their own particular needs, but these are not limited to only home or work. The context given in the question will require you to think and apply.

Home – a **network** is used to allow multiple computers to connect to the internet. It can also be used to stream music and videos around the house and allow files, such as photographs or music, to be accessed. A central data store can be established with videos, pictures and music and all computers can access it. Printing can also be centralised.

Work – at work the key is management and collaboration. Work files can be shared and teams can work on them. Printing can be centralised and management features such as anti virus and backup can be conducted and monitored. A network can be used to monitor and record users actions as well as provide security to files.

Exam questions

1 Describe how a family might make use of a home wireless network. [*6 marks*]

2 Explain how the management could make use of a network at work. [*4 marks*]

Examiner hints and tips

Think about the following in relation to the questions on the left.

Question 1: You can give two in-depth descriptions or three broad ones. Make sure the answer is about the use by the family.

Question 2: Identify, exemplify and then give a reason why this is an advantage/disadvantage to the management.

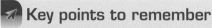

4.4 Limitations of ICT

Specification reference

3.3.4c – explain the limitations of using ICT in society today and how advances in technology may overcome some of those limitations.

Key points to remember

- The limitations are of the technology – what is wrong with it now, what can it not do.
- The advances in technology being developed to overcome some of these limitations.

Keyword

Moore's Law: the observation that the number of transistors on a computer chip doubles approximately every two years. This has been the guiding principle of the ICT industry since it was coined by Intel co-founder Gordon Moore in 1965.

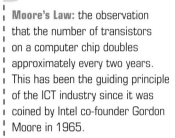

■ Battery life

The battery life on devices is related to their use – the less you use the device, the longer the battery will last. Devices that are meant to be used a lot, such as smart phones, PDAs and laptops have very poor battery life (for example, seven hours of video playback – not enough for a long journey without a recharge).

Longer life batteries and components that use less energy are constantly evolving and the ability to charge without direct connection has just been developed.

Weblink

http://www.crn.com/storage/18841 882;jsessionid=QTJN2TR2T5VL1QE 1GHPSKH4ATMY32JVN

Article about limits to computer data storage.

■ Processing power

The more that technology allows us to do, the more we want and the faster we want it. We are not prepared to wait for things to load, we want things to happen the moment we click them. We demand multi-tasking, with multiple applications running and no waiting.

Processing is getting faster and will continue to do so but will never catch up with software development. We will always want more power.

■ Storage capacity

We are storing vast amounts of data – text, photos (in ever greater resolutions), videos in high definition (HD), audio books and television programmes and podcasts. Computers have vast storage capacity but you need double – half for what you have and half for a backup.

Solid state storage is increasing in capacity and reducing in price. There is also a trend to using 'the cloud' – storing data on the internet in a variety of places – Flickr, for example, for photos. The responsibility of backup is then theirs and not yours.

Example of a small computer

Fingerprint recognition

Size of technology

Technology is getting smaller and can be harder to use. Screen size is reducing and web pages do not fit on the screen without scrolling, which can be wearing on the eyes. Hand-held equipment and netbooks with smaller keypads are harder to use by a population that is getting larger (and sometimes obese).

Bandwidth

Access to and the size of **bandwidth** can both be limiting factors. There is a perceived need to be connected at all times – whether to social networking sites or streaming and downloading video. Linked with speed of response, a high bandwidth is required to make this possible.

Wi-Max is a possible solution as are town-based Wi-Fi networks. There is a need for greater bandwidth and the industry is attempting to provide this. Fixed connection bandwidth is easier to provide than mobile.

Security

With any system there are always those that will try to break into it. Given the amount of data stored on computers, security is a limitation, especially when the weakest point is the end user, not the technology. Security is linked to privacy. The increase in use of cameras and sharing of information makes it easier to invade our privacy. The limitation is the ability of ICT to protect us and guarantee our privacy.

Security issues can never be completely overcome – educating users and producing higher levels of security, use of biometrics, for example, will help but there will always be methods of overcoming it.

Exam questions

1 Explain the limitations of mobile devices for an adult user. [6 marks]

2 Describe how advances in technology can improve security and privacy. [6 marks]

Examiner hints and tips

Think about the following in relation to the questions on the left.

Question 1: This question asks for current problems with mobile devices. The user in the question is important and needs to be addressed in the answer.

Question 2: This question is about new developments and how the limitations can be overcome. Two descriptions in depth or three in less depth are required.

4.5 Distributed databases

Specification reference

3.3.4e – explain how databases may be stored in more than one physical location and how distribution may be carried out using different approaches: partitioned between sites (vertical and horizontal), entire databases duplicated at each site, central database with remote local indexes.

Keywords

Database: a collection of information that is structured in some way. It does not have to be on a computer.

Distributed database: a single logical database that is spread physically across computers in multiple locations that are connected by data communication links.

Weblink

http://msdn.microsoft.com/en-us/ library/ms178148.aspx

Summary of partitioning.

Key points to remember

- You need to know what distribution is and the different types of distribution.
- The next two sections are also related to distributed databases.

Data does not have to be stored in the same location as it is used. In an organisation with many offices, each office will need access to data. Where many locations require access to the same **database** (not necessarily the same data) then a **distributed database** is used.

■ Duplication

This is where each location that requires data has an entire copy of the database at its own location.

■ Central database with local indexes

An index is a data structure that works like the index in a book. It contains references to the data that allow it to be looked up and accessed quickly.

The database is held in a central location and the indexes, either those specific to a particular office/shop or all of them, are held locally. This allows each individual location to perform processing locally and to use the central database for retrieval of a specific record.

■ Partitioning

This is where parts of the data are stored at different locations. No single location stores all the data. There are two types of partitioning: vertical and horizontal.

Record	Inital	Name
1	A	Green
2	B	Yellow
3	C	White
4	D Blue	

Horizontal (row 2)

Vertical

Vertical partitioning

This is where the data is partitioned based on individual fields. You end up with a new table that contains only the fields that are required and an additional table containing those fields that are not required. An office, for example, may only be given access to certain fields within the data. For example, pay fields may not be accessible. Normalisation is a type of vertical partitioning.

Product ID	Description	Supplier ID	Supplier
1	Pen	1	Jones
2	Paper	2	Lead
3	Card	1	Jones

Product ID	Description	Supplier ID
1	Pen	1
2	Paper	2
3	Card	1

Supplier ID	Supplier
1	Jones
2	Lead

The new tables contain only some of the fields of the original.

Horizontal partitioning

This is where the data is partitioned based on records. The data is split into different tables and each table contains exactly the same structure. However, each table will contain different rows. This can be used where only certain people/offices need data that is relevant to them.

Name	Year
Joe Green	7
Paulina White	7
Anne Blue	8
Mike Black	8

Name	Year
Joe Green	7
Paulina White	7

Name	Year
Anne Blue	8
Mike Black	8

This is a list of all the people in a school (shortened) that is run over different sites.

A head of year wants only the year on their site – the database can be partitioned.

The data structure remains the same, it is the records that are different.

Examiner hints and tips

Think about the following in relation to the questions on the left.

Question 1: This question asks for a description of horizontal partitioning but within context.

Question 2: This question requires a learnt response. Examples relevant to partitioning would be useful.

Exam questions

1 Using examples, describe how horizontal partitioning could be used in a business that has shops in different parts of the country. [4 marks]

2 Within the context of database partitioning, describe what is meant by an index. [4 marks]

Use of distributed databases

Specification reference

3.3.4f – discuss the use of different types of distributed database systems.

 Key point to remember

- Although there are generic comparisons, each type of partitioning has its own advantages and disadvantages as well.

 Keywords

Communication link: the method by which data is transferred – broadband, satellite, etc.

Data integrity: making sure that the data is complete and whole.

Data consistency: all copies of the data held are the same – one is not out of sequence with the rest.

Record locking: the technique of preventing simultaneous access to data in a database, to prevent inconsistent results.

Comparison

Any comparison between partitioning methods needs to have a series of criteria:

- **Speed** – how quick is it to run queries and obtain the data that is required.

- **Security** – keeping the data secure, backed up and maintaining the integrity/consistency of the data.

- **Flexibility** – changing the data structure and queries to meet the needs of the organisation.

- Storage space required and **communication links**.

Duplicated

Speed is high because of local access.

Security is down to the individual locations – multiple copies of the data give multiple access points. Backing up is the responsibility of individuals but there are multiple copies if something goes wrong.

Data integrity and **consistency** are a major problem as a change in one database needs to be reflected throughout all of them. There are also more potential points of access for viruses.

Every location needs a complete copy of the database – this increases the amount of storage and backup space required. Communication links are required to perform updates to each site. If the link is down, the integrity and consistency of the data suffers.

Local index

Where a local index exists speed is relatively high. Only data is transferred, no processing is required centrally. If the query/report is not available locally, then the speed is slower. Security is high as only the indexes are stored locally. The main data is at one location. Backup is centralised.

Record locking

There are issues to do with **record locking** – if two locations attempt to change the same data at the same time, it is possible for an incorrect version to be stored.

List partitioning

Southern sales region
Kent
Sussex
Surrey

Eastern sales region
Norfolk
Suffolk
Essex

Northern sales region
Yorkshire
Lancashire
Cumbria

Range partitioning

January and February

March and April

May and June

July and August

Hash partitioning

h1
h2
h3
h4

Types of partitioning

For example, two bank employees attempt to update the same bank account for two different transactions. Employee A and employee B both copy the account's current balance at the same time. Employee A applies one transaction and saves the new balance. Employee B applies a different transaction and saves a new balance that overwrites the information saved by employee A. The balance no longer includes the first transaction and is inaccurate.

Opening balance: £100

Employee A inputs £40 debit   Balance should now be £60

Employee B inputs £25 debit (from opening balance of £100)

Final Balance: £75   Closing balance should be £35

Integrity and consistency are higher in centralised databases – the central store for the data means that there is only one instance. It is also easier to secure against viruses.

The central location has a large storage requirement; the local offices only store the indexes. With regards to communication, there is a large amount of data passing between the central storage and the offices and if the line fails, no data can be received.

Partitioned

Where data is stored locally, because of local access, speed is high. If the data required is held in a different location then the speed decreases.

Security is down to individual locations. Some data will be stored in multiple locations. Multiple copies of the data give multiple access points but to gain all of the data, different sites need to be broken into. Backing up is the responsibility of individuals. It may be possible to recreate the data from different sites if there is an incident but this is not an absolute.

Integrity and consistency are a major problem as a change in one database needs to be reflected throughout the rest. There are also more points of access for viruses.

The amount of storage required differs at each location. Communication links are required to perform updates to each site. If a link is down, the integrity and consistency of the data suffers.

Exam questions

1 Explain the advantages of using a duplicated distributed database system. [6 marks]

2 Compare the security issues of partitioned and local index distributed database systems. [3 marks]

Examiner hints and tips

Think about the following in relation to the questions on the left.

Question 1: This question requires a learnt response. Focus on the reason why they are an advantage.

Question 2: This is a comparison question. Three comparisons are required focusing on security issues.

Security of distributed databases

Specification reference

3.3.4g – explain security issues of distributed databases: interception of data, physical access to data, consistency and integrity of data and describe methods of overcoming these issues.

Keyword

Physical security: systems that prevent an individual, in person, accessing the data.

Key points to remember

- You need to know both the security issue and how to resolve it.
- There is a difference between access to data and being able to use data.

Different types of distributed databases have different issues. Duplicated databases have the entire contents at each site. Local index databases have a central repository – this gives a central point where all the data can be obtained from. Partitioned databases only have elements of the data at each site and to obtain all the data, more than one security breach needs to be made.

Physical security systems

Interception of data

This is the acquisition of data, by a third party, whilst it is being sent from one location to another. All distributed databases move data between themselves and this gives an opportunity for interception.

It includes collecting packets of data as they travel through wireless or wired connections as well as electromagnetic leakage from a monitor.

Interception can be prevented by the use of encryption. Whilst this does not prevent the data being intercepted, it does prevent whoever receives the data from understanding it. Electromagnetic leakage can be prevented by using a suitable frame and special paint.

Physical access to data

With data being stored in many different places in a partitioned database there are many avenues to gaining access to the data. Whilst one location might have good security measures in place, others might be lax.

Preventing physical access to data is about preventing the individual from getting to the terminal. This can be done by security guards patrolling, access control on entrances and locks on doors. There are also software guards such as logon screens and passwords that prevent an intruder, who does get to a terminal, from accessing data.

Data can also be encrypted and passwords placed onto the software itself.

Weblinks

http://www.howstuffworks.com/encryption.htm

How encryption works.

http://www.paypal.com/cgi-bin/webscr?cmd=p/gen/verification-faq-outside

PayPal verification facts and questions.

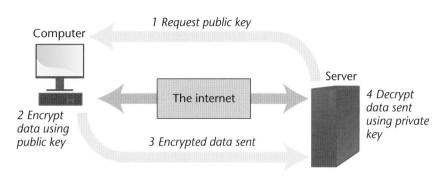

Encryption over the internet

■ Consistency and integrity

This was mentioned briefly in the previous section.

Integrity ensures that data is complete and whole. If incomplete data is entered then this can have an impact down the line – for example, if only half a telephone number is entered or a postcode but no house name/number is entered, then contact becomes difficult.

Integrity is maintained by controlling data entry. Data entered needs to be validated and verified. Validation ensures data conforms to rules – such as length, type, range and presence and gives confidence that the data is sensible and reasonable. Verification ensures that data entered is the same as the source. Neither can ensure accuracy and therefore integrity of the data completely.

Consistency ensures that where more than one copy of the same database is stored, the data is always the same. So, for example, if one office changes a customers details, any other office that also holds those details gets them updated as well.

In vertical partitioning databases, this is done through the use of primary and foreign keys and can be enforced through referential integrity and cascade updates and deletions. In horizontal partitioning databases, if all the data (records) are stored at single locations, then these are easy to maintain. If the same data is duplicated then it becomes more difficult and record locking systems are required.

With local index databases, data is stored centrally and with duplicated databases a record locking system is required.

Exam questions

1 Explain, using examples, how consistency is a problem for duplicated distributed databases. *[6 marks]*

2 Describe how problems with physical access to data could be overcome. *[4 marks]*

Examiner hints and tips

Think about the following in relation to the questions on the left.

Question 1: You must use examples of how consistency is not kept – this question is not about the solution but the problem.

Question 2: This question requires a straight learning response – focus on the solution. Before giving a solution, you must first mention which problem to do with physical access you are talking about.

4.8 Expert systems

Specification reference

3.3.4h – explain what is meant by an expert system and describe its components and applications.

Keyword

Expert: a person with particular in-depth knowledge in a limited area.

Weblink

http://www.pcai.com/web/ai_info/ expert_systems.html

Expert systems.

Key points to remember

■ Expert systems have three components – learn them.

■ The applications are rule-based and can give a reasoned decision.

■ Components

Expert systems are computer programs that are made up of a set of rules that analyse information about a specific type of problem. They can also provide a recommended course of action in order to solve the problem. They attempt to reproduce the decision-making process.

The range of an expert system is very narrow. Each expert system concentrates only on a specific area. Expert systems are designed to replace the 'human expert' – they will attempt to ask similar questions and give the same responses as would be given by a human with expertise in that area.

An expert system is made up of three main parts:

■ the knowledge base.

■ the reasoning, or inference, engine.

■ the user interface – the method by which the user communicates with the expert system.

(LPS) Logical Programming Systems

Products   Support   Download   **About us**   News   Search

Pesticide system

Pests

☐ Red spider mite	A small arachnid.
☐ Caterpillar	The larvae of moths and butterflies.
☐ Aphid	A small fly.
☐ Slug	A mollusc.

Pesticide expert system

Weblink

http://www.it.bton.ac.uk/staff/lp22/
CS237/CS237MedicalXSys.html

Medical expert systems.

Knowledge base

The knowledge base of expert systems contains both factual and heuristic knowledge.

Factual knowledge is the knowledge of the specific area that is widely shared, typically found in textbooks or journals.

Heuristic knowledge is the knowledge that is acquired through experience and reasoning. It is the knowledge that underpins the 'art of good guessing'.

Inference engine

An inference engine asks the end user questions and based on their answers will follow lines of logic. This may lead to more questions and ultimately to an answer.

An inference engine is based on rules. A rule consists of an IF part and a THEN part (also called a condition and an action).

The IF part lists a set of conditions. If the IF part of the rule is satisfied, the THEN part can be concluded. This may be the answer, or a new set of rules.

At a basic level an inference engine can be seen as a tree.

Applications of expert systems are in areas of focused knowledge and usually based around troubleshooting – car maintenance, health and technical troubleshooting are common applications. Anything with rules can be made into an expert system, for example, pension calculations and finding the best type of computer for you.

Exam questions

1 Describe what is meant by an expert system   [*4 marks*]

2 Describe the **three** components of an expert system. [*6 marks*]

Examiner hints and tips

Think about the following in relation to the above questions.

Question 1: This question requires a learnt response – give the definition.

Question 2: Again, a learnt response, with three marks for identifying the components and three more for exemplifying your answer.

Decision making

Specification reference

3.3.4i – describe how the following ICT tools can be used to assist decision making: management information systems (MIS) and expert systems.

🔑 Keyword

Decision making: the outcome of a process leading to a specific action.

Weblink

http://www.bestpricecomputers. co.uk/glossary/management-information-system.htm

Explanation of management information systems.

Employee by salary

Exam questions

1 How can an expert system help a company relocate its business?
[*4 marks*]

2 Describe how a MIS can be used to help a company ascertain whether a marketing campaign was successful. [*4 marks*]

⚡ Key points to remember

■ Exam questions will ask for how the systems are used, not descriptions of them.

■ Both systems are only as good as the data that is input into them.

■ Management information systems (MIS)

These are systems that collect, process and produce reports. They can summarise the data they have collected in an easy-to-understand way – for example, tabular or graphical.

They can assist in **decision making** by presenting specific data, for example, sales trends, customer orders, etc. They can also organise financial information – for example, expenditure v income analysis or reports on best sellers, overdue accounts and demographics.

■ Expert system

Expert systems contain expert knowledge and rules so questions can be asked and a solution with reasoning suggested.

These systems help decision making by providing a conclusion – an action to take based on the available information. They can give managers a reasoned conclusion as to why a particular action is the best to take. Usually, this is only a starting point as there may be additional information unknown to the system.

Both systems can save time and labour costs.

Examiner hints and tips

Think about the following in relation to the questions on the left.

Question 1: This question asks for the questions that could be asked of an expert system to find the right response.

Question 2: This is a contextual question – it asks for the reports that can be produced to assist in answering the questions raised.

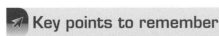

4.10

Digital television

 Specification reference

3.3.4j – discuss the range of services offered by digital television networks and the impact of these services on individuals, television companies and broadcasters.

 Keyword

Digital television: a way of transmitting TV pictures and sound as computerised bits of information.

Weblinks

http://www.bbc.co.uk/digital/tv/tv_interactive.shtml

BBC digital television.

http://www.crtc.gc.ca/eng/publications/reports/interactive_tv.htm

Canadian report on interactive television services.

Key points to remember

■ Digital television is in addition to analogue television.
■ The services that are available on the red button.

■ Range of services

Digital television services include information services – for example, TV guides and the ability to schedule a series to record (also provided on analogue). Some systems include video games and paying for content such as movies on demand and voting on reality shows.

Services also include being able to change the camera angle, select different languages or even choose different endings to programmes.

Some services are broadcast to the user (for example, camera angles) and others make use of telephone lines to send data back (for example, as voting systems).

■ Impact of services

The three main areas of impact are on the individual watching the programmes, the company producing the programmes and the broadcaster who is delivering the service/programmes to the end user.

Digital television provides the end user with interactivity and services on demand. For the company, it is about providing a service that will generate the most income and gaining feedback to improve the service. For the broadcaster, it is about providing features that will enable them to gain more subscribers and therefore increase advertising revenue.

Examiner hints and tips

Think about the following in relation to the questions on the left.

Question 1: This question requires your answer to focus on why your point is an advantage to the viewer. You must make at least two points – three would be better.

Question 2: Your answer should be a description of the services contextualised to making money for the broadcaster. You do not need to say how they make money but if you did it would ensure the mark as it shows your thinking process.

Exam questions

1 Explain the advantages to the viewer of digital television. [6 marks]

2 Describe **two** services offered by digital television that can be used by the broadcaster to increase revenue. [4 marks]

Internal resources

Specification reference

3.3.4k – describe the internal resources of a system: human, technological and accommodation.

Keyword

Internal resources: internal means within the system that has been defined. This is within a specific boundary – it may be within an organisation, or within a part of the organisation as a sub-system.

Key points to remember

■ The context of the question will allow you to give examples of the internal resources to expand your answer.

■ The system may be the whole system or it may be a sub-system.

Human – these are all the employees who are involved in some way with the system. They could be contractors or permanent staff.

Technological – these are the ICT resources that exist within the system – the hardware and software required for the organisation to do its job. It is NOT the component parts of a computer, but may include the computer itself.

Accommodation – these are the buildings, the furniture and anything not covered by human and technological resources.

Personnel resources of a supermarket

Accommodation resources of a system – the building, car park and vehicles

Examiner hints and tips

Think about the following in relation to the questions on the left.

Question 1: This question requires a learnt response. Your answer should focus on identifying and describing two different types of accommodation.

Question 2: This question is contextualised – you need to think of three different technological resources that a supermarket would have – identify, expand and give an example of their use for full marks.

Exam questions

1 Describe **two** different accommodation resources of a system. [4 marks]

2 Describe the technological internal resources of a supermarket. [6 marks]

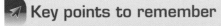
 4.12 **Exchange of information**

Specification reference

3.3.4I – explain the importance of ensuring that information is exchanged accurately and in a timely manner within an organisation and describe how this is achieved.

 Keyword

Information:
Data + Context + Structure. Data needs to be placed within context to be turned into information.

Key points to remember

- The importance will be contextualised to the scenario in the exam question.
- There are two elements – why they are important and how they are achieved.

■ Accuracy

The accuracy of **information** is important as it is relied on by other people further down the line. If information is not accurate, it cannot be used with confidence. Remember from AS, there are seven factors affecting the quality of information.

■ Timely manner

This is whether the information has been received in time for it to be of value and use. This is, again, one of the seven factors affecting the quality of information.

■ How achieved

Accuracy is achieved by validation, verification and checking the source. Neither validation nor verification can ensure accuracy (as you learnt at AS). It is very difficult to ensure complete accuracy. There are computer methods to ensure verification – a check digit, for example, but if the original data is not accurate, the received data will not be accurate.

Information is exchanged in a timely manner by using electronic communication in place of paper, internal systems that can automate the flow of electronic information and manual procedures that can move paperwork around as required.

Exam questions

1 Explain why information between a supermarket till and a stock control system needs to be transferred accurately. [*4 marks*]

2 Describe how the transfer of information in a timely manner can be achieved between a supermarket till and a stock control system. [*4 marks*]

Examiner hints and tips

Think about the following in relation to the questions on the left.

Question 1: This question is contextualised to a supermarket and the accurate transfer of data. Use examples in your answer.

Question 2: This question focuses on how the transfer of information can be achieved in a timely manner. Your answer should say how electronic communication is faster than paper.

4.13

Characteristics of systems

Specification reference

3.3.4m – describe the characteristics of the following systems: personnel, finance and stock control.

Key points to remember

- Characteristics of systems are different to the purpose.
- Characteristics are the inputs, processes, outputs and storage to the system.

Keywords

Personnel systems: dealing with employees and storing data relevant to them and their time in the organisation. Also known as human resources (HR).

Income and expenditure: income – money coming in; expenditure – money going out.

Weblink

http://www.
computersinpersonnelhr.com/
products/ciphr-people/ciphr-
people.htm

Example of an HR personnel system.

■ Personnel systems

These are systems that store information on the employees within an organisation.

The system will store:

- Name and address.
- Personal details: date of birth, NI number, salary, attendance.
- Job details: date appointed, job title, promotion record.
- Courses completed.

They can be linked to the finance system for salaries and pension, and be updated when the employee completes courses, moves house, etc.

The personnel system can also match employees skills, with those required for specific jobs within the organisation.

■ Finance systems

These are systems that manage the money within an organisation. There are three aspects of finance systems – money coming in, money going out and future predictions.

Organisations are paid for their products or services. The finance system will have a record of customers and how much they have been invoiced for. When the customer pays, the system will record this against the invoice. The system will also produce statements and generate requests for overdue payments. The system will perform basic mathematics – adding VAT, for example.

The system will also pay the bills that the organsiation generates. These will be cross referenced against an order.

Most finance systems produce reports of **income** against **expenditure** and can predict expenditure based on past records and known variables, such as advertising campaigns and expansion.

Weblink

http://www.businesslink.gov.uk/ bdotg/action/detail?type=RESOURCE S&itemId=1073792781

List of stock control features.

Stock control device

■ Stock control systems

Stock is the quantity of physical items held by a company or organisation – it can be components that are used to manufacture products or products themselves.

Stock control systems hold details of the stock, the supplier and mininum stock level and reorder amounts. They can be linked into an ordering system and as customers place orders, the stock level will be adjusted. When stock reaches a predefined level, more stock can be ordered (and the order note tied into the finance system). When stock arrives, the system will be updated (and the invoice released for payment).

These systems can produce reports on the amount of stock held and predict the amount required based on previous records and external events, such as advertising campaigns (which should increase orders).

Stock control systems can make use of radio frequency identification (RFID) tags to record items.

Exam questions

1 Describe the characteristics of a personnel system.   [*4 marks*]

2 Describe how a stock control system and a finance system are interrelated.   [*4 marks*]

Examiner hints and tips

Think about the following in relation to the above questions.

Question 1: This question requires a straightforward learnt response. Identify, expand and exemplify two different aspects to get full marks.

Question 2: This question is looking for the characteristics of one that link into the characteristics of the other. Your answer could focus on order notes and delivery notes for stock – allowing finds to be allocated to a supplier and then paid on receipt of the goods.

5 Implementing computer-based information systems

Client involvement

 Specification reference

3.3.5a – describe the involvement of the client when a custom-written computer-based information system is to be produced, from the initial meeting with the client to the installation of the system.

Key point to remember

- The client must be involved at every stage of the development of a custom-written information system.

Client involvement

- The client will need to provide details of what the new system should do.

- These details form the basis on which the development will take place.

- If the details are either incomplete or inaccurate, then the final system may not fully meet the needs of the client and could be a waste of time and money.

- If the client is consulted at all stages then errors, inaccuracies and omissions should be prevented.

- During consultation, developers should listen to any concerns, provide opportunities to suggest modifications or raise any concerns about any inaccuracies.

- The methodology being used will dictate the extent of the client involvement during the development of the system.

- Irrespective of the methodology used, the developer must ensure that the client is consulted at each stage.

Exam question

1 Describe the importance of a client being involved during the development of a custom-written system.
[*4 marks*]

Examiner hints and tips

Think about the following in relation to the question on the left.

The question requires you to describe the importance of a client being involved. In your answer, you will need to consider the importance of a client being involved and also the impact of a client not being involved during the development of the system.

5.2 Decisions about upgrading

Specification reference

3.3.5c – explain how the expertise of staff, costs, benefits and current systems affect decisions about upgrading or installing software and hardware.

Keyword

Cost–benefit analysis: an analysis of the cost effectiveness of different alternatives in order to see whether the benefits outweigh the costs.

Key point to remember

- The decision about whether to upgrade or install new software and hardware should be taken during the analysis stage of the system life cycle.

A **cost–benefit analysis** should be completed with the results influencing the decision. Costs to be considered include:

- If the software and hardware are being upgraded then staff are likely to have some of the skills to use the software and hardware and will require little, if any, training but if new hardware and software are being installed then more training will be needed.

- Licences for new or upgraded software.

- New software must run successfully on the old system. The hardware may need to be upgraded to meet the new requirements.

- Obsolete or outdated hardware may need replacing. Additionally, new hardware may require changes to the software being used.

Other issues that will have to be considered, and decisions made, include the method of implementation and the available timescale.

The upgrading or installing of a system must, ultimately, ensure that the benefits of the new outweigh those of the old. In addition, the long-term benefits need to outweigh the costs and inconvenience/disruption of the installation.

Exam question

1 Describe how hardware can affect a decision about the upgrading of software. [4 marks]

Examiner hints and tips

Think about the following in relation to the above question.

The question requires you to focus on the relationship between hardware and software. You should consider the hardware currently in place and then make some reference to the implications of having to purchase new hardware as a result of needing to upgrade the software.

5.3 Selecting, implementing and supporting solutions

Specification reference

3.3.5b – discuss the implications of selecting, implementing and supporting the installation of custom-written and off-the-shelf solutions.

Keywords

Custom-written software: software developed to meet the specified needs and requirements of an organisation.

Off-the-shelf software: software which can be purchased, installed and used immediately.

Key points to remember

- The selection of either custom-written or off-the-shelf software will depend on many factors.
- During the implementation and installation of software the staff that will be using it will need to be involved.

The main features that should be considered when deciding whether to install a **custom-written** or **off-the-shelf software** solution are shown in the table below:

Feature	Off-the-shelf	Custom-written
Cost	▪ Either a one-off cost or a yearly rental cost. ▪ May be thousands of pounds plus additional costs for each station it is used on.	▪ Need to hire the company/person to write the software which could cost many thousands of pounds. ▪ The end user owns the software and can sell it to recoup some of the development cost.
Support	▪ Discussion groups, online help, books and training courses.	▪ Only likely to get support from the people who write the software – problems may arise if they choose not to support it or go out of business.
Purpose	▪ May have to be altered and edited to fit the purpose. May never meet the purpose precisely. ▪ Will have many additional features that may or may not be used.	▪ Will fit the purpose precisely and do exactly what was asked. Possible problems may arise if the analysis was wrong. ▪ If something is not specified it will not be in the final product.
Testing	▪ Will have been tested by many individuals. Bug fixes will be released regularly by the company.	▪ Will have been only tested by a few people and there may be many bugs. Correcting them will take time.
Availability	▪ Immediately available.	▪ Will take time (may be a few months) to complete the analysis, etc.
Choice	▪ Choice between packages available – but none may be an exact fit.	▪ There is choice of who to get to write the software and the end user will have significant influence over the final product.
Upgrade	▪ Likely to use a standard file format and the company is likely to release upgraded products.	▪ New printers and drivers for peripherals may not be supported and major upgrades might not happen.
Upgrade	▪ Support for new peripherals and operating systems as standard.	▪ If the software does not use a recognised file format it may not be possible to upgrade.
New staff	▪ May well be familiar with the new software.	▪ Unlikely to be familiar with the new software.
Footprint	▪ Large footprint.	▪ Small footprint.

■ Implementing and supporting the installation of custom-written and off-the-shelf software

The impact on staff

- Some staff may feel that the introduction of new software may lead to job losses or that they do not have the skills required to use the software.

- Staff should be offered training sessions to ensure that they are able to use the software confidently.

- The benefits of new software and reassurance that staff will not lose their jobs should be stressed during installation.

- Staff should have access to user guides and documentation to help them use the software effectively.

The impact on customers/clients of the organisation

- It may be that, despite testing during the development of the software, some teething problems are still present with the software.

- This may mean that, for example, incorrect invoices are sent out or details are not transferred to the new system correctly.

- If this happens, an explanation should be given to the customers and issues corrected as quickly as possible.

The implementation and installation of software should be managed carefully, with the needs of the staff and customers of the organisation considered as much as possible. By doing this, there should be no loss of confidence in the organisation from either the staff or customers.

Exam question

1 Explain the implications of selecting off-the-shelf software over custom-written software.
[*8 marks*]

Examiner hints and tips

Think about the following in relation to the question on the left.

The focus of this question is on the selection of off-the-shelf software over custom-written software. You should consider why off-the-shelf software should be selected and explain why this would be beneficial. You should attempt to cover as many of the features, given in the table above, as you can.

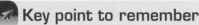

5.4 Installation methods

Specification reference

3.3.5d – describe a range of methods for installing a new computer-based information system: parallel, phased, direct, pilot.

Key point to remember

- There are four strategies that can be used to install a system.

Parallel

With this strategy, the old and new systems are run concurrently. The results from each are compared for accuracy and consistency. The old system is not discarded until there is complete confidence in the reliability and accuracy of the new system.

Phased

Different systems, within an organisation, are brought online one by one. Initially, only selected sections use the new system. Once confidence in the new system is high, then other sections start to use the new system. This continues until the whole organisation is using the new system.

Pilot

This strategy requires selected sections to use the new system or specific tasks to be completed using the new system. The rest of the tasks are completed using the old system. Once confidence in the new system is high, then another task is completed using the new system. This continues until all the tasks within an organisation are completed using the new system.

Direct

The new system completely replaces the old system, on a given day, with no interim parallel, phased or pilot implementation. This is probably the riskiest implementation strategy and is also known as the 'big bang' method.

Exam question

1 Describe the following implementation methods:

a direct　　　[2 marks]

b parallel.　　[2 marks]

Examiner hints and tips

Think about the following in relation to the question on the left.

The question requires you to describe two implementation methods – you should focus your answer on these. There are two marks available for each method.

5.5 Choosing an installation method

Specification reference

3.3.5e – discuss the choice of a particular installation method or methods for a range of applications.

Key point to remember

■ The choice of installation method will be based on the advantages and disadvantages of each method.

Method	Advantages	Disadvantages
Parallel	■ If a problem is found with the new system it is possible for the organisation to function as the old system is still in place and can be used. ■ There is little or no detrimental effect on an organisation.	■ Data is duplicated. ■ Staff undertake tasks twice. ■ Inconsistencies have to be checked and errors have to be located.
Phased	■ If a problem or bug is found with the new system the organisation can still function using the old system. ■ Limits the detrimental effect on an organisation.	■ The potential for doubling workload if data or information moves departments during processing. ■ Increased workload for staff. ■ Implementation can take a long time. ■ Very expensive in terms of staff and time costs.
Pilot	■ If a problem or bug is found with the new system, these can be rectified before implementation is continued. ■ Limits the dertrimental effect on an organisation.	■ Tasks that do not work in the new system at the start may be those causing the major problems in the old system. ■ Implementation can take a long time. ■ Very expensive in terms of staff and time costs.
Direct	■ Cheapest in terms of staff and time costs.	■ Problems or bugs may lead to complete loss of data and/or the potential failure of the organisation.

Exam question

1 Explain the factors that should be considered when selecting the parallel implementation method. **[6 marks]**

Examiner hints and tips

Think about the following in relation to the question on the left.

The question requires you to explain the factors involved in deciding to use the parallel method. You should provide the advantages and disadvantages of this method in your answer.

5.6 **Role of reviews**

 Specification reference

3.3.5f – explain the role of reviews during the life of a computer-based information system, describing how reviews may be planned for and carried out effectively.

Key point to remember

- During the life of any system, reviews need to be undertaken to ensure that the system continues to operate effectively.

Keywords

External changes: relate to legislation changes such as tax and VAT and data protection updates. External changes will require changes to the system.

Internal changes: relate to the organisation, for example, a change in the mode of operation whereby new functions performed by the system will need to be included.

■ Role of reviews

- Reviews should be scheduled to occur on a regular basis. This ensures that the system continues to provide satisfactory levels of performance to the users.

- By notifying users of the system when reviews occur, users can report problems as soon as they happen.

- Regular reviews can also ensure that the system does not become out of date.

- Reviews can be scheduled to coincide with any planned **external** and/or **internal changes** in the operation of the organisation using the system.

- Reviews enable hardware and software developments to be incorporated into a system. Reviews should also take place to ensure that the new hardware and software works successfully with the system.

- During a review, users should be asked for their views on how well the system is performing. As they are using the system, they should be able to provide valuable feedback on the overall performance.

Exam question

1 Explain the role of reviews during the life of a computer-based information system. [4 marks]

Examiner hints and tips

Think about the following in relation to the above question.

The question requires you to explain the role of reviews during the life of a system. You should consider the scheduling of reviews, user/client involvement and how the results of the review can be used to improve the system.

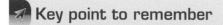

Maintenance methods

Specification reference

3.3.5g – describe perfective, adaptive and corrective maintenance.

> ### Key point to remember
>
> ■ There are three types of maintenance that can be carried out: perfective, adaptive and corrective.

 **Keyword**

Maintenance: the process of ensuring that a software system/ product continues to meet the needs of the end users.

■ Adaptive

This type of **maintenance** usually occurs when the organisation using the system has a new need that the system must fulfil. The system may need to be adapted due to changes within the organisation using it, external changes such as legislation (for example, tax/VAT rate changes) or to enable the system to operate with new hardware.

■ Perfective

This type of maintenance usually occurs when it may be advantageous to make changes to enhance the performance of the system or to make it easier for the end users to use. It should turn a good system into a better one. This type of maintenance is generally completed at the request of the end users. The overall functionality of the system is not changed.

■ Corrective

Corrective maintenance is also known as remedial maintenance. This type of maintenance is usually completed if there are errors in the software. These errors or 'bugs' can be of two types: programming or logic.

Exam question

1 Identify and describe **one** maintenance method.   [*3 marks*]

Examiner hints and tips

Think about the following in relation to the above question.

> The question requires you to identify and then describe one maintenance method. You need to identify the method for the first mark – if you don't get this mark you will not be able to get the other two allocated marks.

5.8 Need for maintenance

Specification reference

3.3.5h – explain the need for perfective, adaptive and corrective maintenance during the life of a computer-based information system.

 Key point to remember

■ Over the life of a system, maintenance will need to be carried out. What needs to be done will determine the type of maintenance that is carried out.

The main reasons for post-implementation maintenance and the type of maintenance used to resolve them are:

■ Errors/bugs that may not have been identified during the testing process become apparent when the system is being used – corrective.

■ The rewriting of procedures to reduce the response time of the system – perfective.

■ After a period of using the system, users may find that parts of the system are not working as they would like – perfective.

■ Tasks that were not included at the design stage now need to be incorporated into the system – perfective.

■ Security issues may emerge that mean the system requires an extra level of protection – adaptive.

■ The software developer may find a way to make the system run more efficiently – this will usually result in the release of a patch/ fix – corrective.

■ New hardware or software may be purchased which needs to be integrated into the existing system – adaptive.

■ The addition of short-cut keys to help the end users carry out processes – perfective.

Exam question

1 Explain why corrective maintenance would be carried out on a system. [*4 marks*]

Examiner hints and tips

Think about the following in relation to the above question.

The question requires you to explain why corrective maintenance needs to be carried out. Your answer does not need to include a description of corrective maintenance.

6.1 Consultation and participation

Specification reference

3.3.6c – discuss the importance of consultation, participation and communication when managing change.

Keywords

Consultation: asking others for their opinion.

Participation: the act of sharing ideas and getting involved in making decisions.

Communication: informing people of decisions – letting them know what is happening.

Weblink

http://www.business.vic.gov.
au/busvicwr/_assets/main/
lib60037/08_hpt3-1employeepartic
ipationindecision.pdf

Employee participation in decision making.

Key points to remember

- Managing change is related to the introduction of a new system of change to procedures and processes.
- There is a degree of crossover – consultation involves participation and all require communication.

Three important elements of change management that can be used to minimise the disruption and allow the organisation to utilise the support of the workforce are: **consultation**, **participation** and **communication**.

Consultation – the greater the number of relevant people that are consulted, the greater the information that will be available for developing change plans. Any individuals who have contributed will have a greater commitment to making change work if some of their own suggestions have been included. However, the more people you ask, the greater the number of different ideas you will be given. Some ideas will inevitably conflict which means some people's suggestions will not be taken up – this may lead to resentment.

Participation – this is getting everyone involved and giving them ownership of the process and product. It can include being involved in analysis, design, reviews and testing.

Communication – change that occurs without communication is doomed to failure from the start. Communication must be continuous and relevant – there should be no secrets or surprises.

Exam questions

1 Explain how participation can be used to assist with the introduction of a new system. [6 marks]

2 Explain the importance of consultation when designing a new system. [4 marks]

Examiner hints and tips

Think about the following in relation to the questions on the left.

Question 1: This question is about how participation should be used and why it is an advantage.

Question 2: This question is about the reasons why consultation is important.

6.2 Impact of external change

Specification reference

3.3.6a – discuss the impact of external change on an organisation, individuals within the organisation and on the systems in use.

Keywords

Impact: the effect on one thing of changing another.

Change: when something is done in a different manner to the way it was done before.

Weblink

http://www.shvoong.com/business-management/human-resource-management/1832001-organisational-change-forces-prompting-change/

Summary of forces prompting change.

Key points to remember

■ The focus of this section is not on what the external changes are but the impact of them.

■ External changes are those that occur outside of the boundaries of the system.

The **impact** of external **change** is something happening outside of an organisation that affects the way in which the organisation works.

External changes can include:

■ Financial – for example, interest rates and VAT.

■ Research – for example, production techniques and materials that can be used.

■ Competition – for example, production methods, price cuts and new products.

■ Personal – for example, moving house, getting married, having children or retiring.

External change can also include the building of new roads, houses and shopping centres – all of these things can affect a business.

Impact on organisation

The ultimate impact of external change on an organisation is that it goes out of business. Taxes, competition and legislation can all result in a company closing. Moving back from this, there could be redundancies and restructuring. External change can also be positive – for example, lower taxes or new roads making it easier for customers to reach you. Lower interest rates on loans can result in expansion with new product lines, new areas of business and more customers. This might lead to a growth in employment and restructuring to cope with the new employees and business.

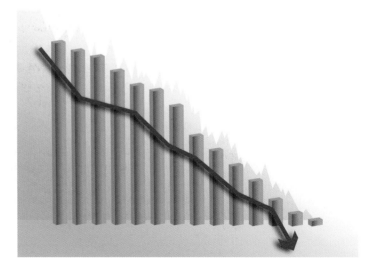

Impact on individuals

If a company fails, then the impact on individuals is going to be redundancy. If a company expands, then there is the possibility of employment. Between these two extremes, there are many impacts. Individuals may have to work part-time, or acquire new skills or be retrained to work on new products or in a different area of an organisation. If a business relocates, then it may be necessary to move house.

External change on individuals can also include events such as births, deaths and marriages. These may have consequences on working overtime, flexitime, teleworking and the job satisfaction that an employee gets.

Impact on systems in use

Systems can be technical – computer-based or mechanical – or they can be administrative. New production methods may require new technology, retraining staff or hiring new personnel.

Systems may be streamlined as a result of a change in the economy or an increase in competition. When systems change, it is either to remove something that is currently in place – procedure or personnel – or to add something new.

Exam questions

1 Explain the impact of new competition on an organisation.
[*6 marks*]

2 Describe the impact that a downturn in the economy can have on individuals within an organisation. [*4 marks*]

Examiner hints and tips

Think about the following in relation to the above questions.

Question 1: This question is about new competition. Competitors may have new products, undercut prices, lure staff away or make use of new production techniques. These are the areas that cause the change – your answer needs to focus on the impact of these on the organisation.

Question 2: A downturn can lead to many impacts – your answer needs to focus on the impacts on individuals.

Change management

Specification reference

3.3.6b – describe change management and factors that must be considered (staff capability, staff views, systems, equipment and accommodation) when managing change.

 Keyword

Capability: the ability to perform actions; an individuals skill in using software.

Weblink

http://www.businessballs.com/changemanagement.htm

Change management.

Key points to remember

- This section is about how to manage the process of change.
- Change is inevitable and is required for a company to survive. Unless it is properly managed, the company may cease to exist.

Change management is a complex process. There are organisations that deal specifically with change and helping firms to change. Change management has several phases (rather like a system life cycle).

Initially there is a source of change. This needs to be evaluated and a decision taken as to whether change is required. The nature of the change must be agreed and communicated to the workforce (if appropriate). The change needs to be planned with goals established. An action plan for the change needs to be drawn up and this should anticipate the effects of the change and how to minimise them. The change then needs to be implemented – this may require a change in culture, removing staff resistance and a change in work practices – depending on the nature of the change. All of this needs to be managed.

■ Staff capability

The workforce must be involved and where appropriate, the skills of the staff should be utilised. Staff need retraining in the use of new systems, changes in procedure or the culture of the organisation.

The change itself will determine how much training is required – and how similar the old and new systems are.

If staff are trained too far in advance of the changeover, they may forget skills. If the training is too close, they may not have time to assimilate the skills. Training takes staff away from their current jobs, which still need to be done, and this needs to be carefully managed.

Staff who have skills that they feel they could offer, but that are not used, can become resistant to the process and need managing.

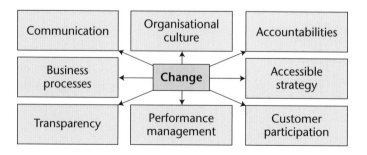

Organisational processes

Staff views

Staff are the individuals who use and know the most about the system. They should be consulted about what needs changing and how to make the changes. They must appear to be valued and their opinions taken on board. Without the backing of the staff, changes will not work. This could include consultation and participation – involvement improves familiarity and reduces resistance to change.

Systems and equipment

If a change is opposed and not welcomed by staff, nothing is worse than the system not working. A system must be thoroughly tested to ensure that it does the job it is supposed to. There are always problems with new systems and new procedures and training staff in the use of new procedures and equipment. Data needs to be transferred and the interfaces between systems and sub-systems established.

The exact date and time of changeover needs to be established and all individuals concerned need to be informed of what is happening and the role they have to play. Too far in advance and a second changeover of data may be required; too close and the pressure may mean it overruns.

Accommodation

New equipment, departments and individuals need places to work. Equipment must be set up and this can involve additional power points, air conditioning and floor space. New departments (such as technical support and maintenance) will need **accommodation** and to be included in the organisational infrastructure.

Exam questions

1 Describe the considerations that must be given to staff views when managing change. [4 marks]

2 Describe the factors that should be considered when managing the changeover of systems and equipment. [6 marks]

Examiner hints and tips

Think about the following in relation to the questions on the left.

Question 1: The focus of your response needs to be on how staff views can be used in managing change – four marks will be awarded for giving two in-depth considerations.

Question 2: Your answer should focus on the timing of data changeover and systems – six marks will be awarded for giving three in-depth answers.

Codes of conduct

Specification reference

3.3.6d – discuss ethics relating to ICT with reference to codes of conduct, for example, the British Computer Society (BCS) code of conduct and the Association for Computing Machinery (ACM) Code of Ethics and Professional Conduct.

 Keyword

Ethics: discussion of right and wrong – encompasses moral behaviour.

Weblinks

http://www.bcs.org/server. php?show=nav.6030

BCS, The Chartered Institute for IT, code of conduct.

http://www.acm.org/about/ code-of-ethics

The Association for Computing Machinery (ACM) Code of Ethics.

 Key points to remember

- Codes of conduct are not legally binding.
- Ethics and codes of conduct work both ways between employer and employees.

Ethics relating to ICT are about the sensible, legal and moral use of ICT. They are about developing and implementing policies that do not take advantage of any individual and utilise technology to the best of its capabilities.

The ethics of a company are usually to be found documented within a code of conduct.

A code of conduct is a non-legislative (not part of the law) set of principles that an organisation draws up that lay down standards in the workplace. They are expectations of mutually agreed behaviour.

Codes of conduct

- Set boundaries for what is expected from an employee. These are not likely to be written explicitly into an employee's contract so are put into a code.

- They establish what can and cannot be done on the computers.

- They give expectations of behaviour – the employee and employer both understand and know the boundaries of behaviour.

- They set out the rights, roles and responsibilities of employees and employers in their actions with each other and with customers.

- They give a framework for disciplinary action if an employee breaks the code of conduct.

- They give the organisation a professional standing within the industry and to its customers.

There are two codes of conduct mentioned in the specification, the BCS and ACM. The web link to both is on the left. Have a look through them and familiarise yourself with the contents.

Examples of statements in codes of conduct include:

- You shall conduct your professional activities without discrimination against clients or colleagues.

- You shall act with integrity in your relationships with all members of the BCS and with members of other professions with whom you work in a professional capacity.

- You shall seek to upgrade your professional knowledge and skill, and shall maintain awareness of technological developments,

Weblink

http://www.businessweek.com/
technology/content/aug2009/
tc20090816_435499.htm

Why be an ethical company?

procedures and standards which are relevant to your field, and encourage your subordinates to do likewise.

■ You shall not claim any level of competence that you do not possess. You shall only offer to do work or provide a service that is within your professional competence.

■ You shall accept professional responsibility for your work and for the work of colleagues who are defined in a given context as working under your supervision.

ICT and ethics are continually changing. A code of conduct, because it is not a specific part of the contract of employment, can be updated to take into consideration the shifting environment and technical nature of ICT.

This can be a disadvantage – with the goalposts and the boundaries ever changing there is no stability. What might have been acceptable one week may not be acceptable the next. Other disadvantages may include a perceived lack of trust in the workforce – having to spell out exactly what is and is not allowed may be like being back at school! Following an ethical policy can put you at a competitive disadvantage – other companies may not follow a code and this may mean they can sell their goods cheaper.

There is, however, a niche market for ethical companies. In ICT, being seen to be 'green' and carbon neutral is important. A company that is ethical is fair and treats its employees and customers with respect. This can gain customers and increase staff loyalty and efficiency.

Exam questions

1 Explain the advantages of a company having a code of conduct. [6 marks]

2 Describe ethical issues that a company should address. [4 marks]

Examiner hints and tips

Think about the following in relation to the above questions.

Question 1: This question requires a straightforward learnt response. Identify, expand on and exemplify two different aspects to get full marks.

Question 2: Your answer should focus on the characteristics of one that link into the characteristics of the other. For example, the use of order notes and delivery notes for stock – allowing finds to be allocated to a supplier and then paid on receipt of the goods.

Activities of professional bodies

Specification reference

3.3.6e – describe the purpose and activities of professional bodies, e.g. the BCS.

BCS

Mission – to enable the information society by promoting change and wider social and economic progress through the advancement of information technology, science and practice.

Vision – to be a world-class organisation for IT. To ensure that our profession has the skills and capabilities to meet the IT demands of a changing world and to ensure that we, as an organisation, are adapting to that world and can continue to grow our impact and influence in the decades ahead.

Values – we pledge to:

- Think ahead and focus on action by putting things in place to meet the future needs of all our stakeholders.

- Be open and work together by sharing best practice and encouraging collaboration between our members, customers and the industry.

- Drive progress and enable change by advancing the role of IT in bettering society, the economy, business and education.

Key points to remember

- Activities include events and publications that the professional bodies produce.
- The BCS promotes wider social and economic progress through the advancement of information technology, science and practice.

A professional body is a formal group that is set up to oversee a particular area of industry.

Professional bodies perform a variety of roles and offer their members many activities:

- They set standards for the workers within the industry. This involves creating a code of conduct that its members must uphold.

- Examinations are provided by the BCS. They set a standard and maintain it. A qualification from the BCS is valued worldwide and recognised by similar bodies in other countries.

- They provide publications and discussion papers on a variety of topics. These enable the members to be up to date.

- They hold conferences where members can meet like-minded individuals and ensure that they are current with any new developments. They can also have an input into legislation and the industry.

- They hold local meetings to allow members to network and share experiences.

Exam questions

1 Describe the purpose of the BCS. *[4 marks]*

2 Describe the activities of the BCS which would make it worthwhile for a network manager to join. *[6 marks]*

Examiner hints and tips

Think about the following in relation to the above questions.

Question 1: This requires a straightforward learnt response. Your answer should identify and expand on two points.

Question 2: This is a contextual question – it is asking for the activities that are relevant to a network manager.

6.6 Advantages and disadvantages of professional bodies

Specification reference

3.3.6f – explain the advantages and disadvantages of belonging to a professional body.

Key point to remember

- The advantages and disadvantages can be to different groups within a company – for example, end users, network manager or management.

Keyword

Professional body: is a group of people in the same occupation who are given the responsibility of maintaining control of the occupation and setting the codes of conduct and guidelines for people working within the occupation.

Advantages

Belonging to a **professional body** gives professional recognition – either by the use of post nominal letters or an email address, for example, @bcs.org. Members are kept up to date with developments in a range of areas and specialist groups can assist with this. Career development, through exams and a training framework, can be mapped to the industry's requirements. There are also financial benefits – cheaper insurance, software and special offers on hardware.

Weblink

http://www.bcs.org.uk

Website for the BCS, The Chartered Institue for IT.

Disadvantages

Being a member of a professional body requires you to follow its code of conduct – this may not always be appropriate. Membership costs money – some people may not be able to afford it. To gain value from membership, a member needs to make use of the training courses, books and conferences. This costs money and time. Where there are rival professional bodies, advertising membership of one may be a disadvantage or limiting.

Exam questions

1 Explain the advantages to a teacher of belonging to the BCS.
[6 marks]

2 Describe the disadvantages to a self-employed programmer of belonging to the BCS.
[6 marks]

Examiner hints and tips

Think about the following in relation to the questions on the left.

Question 1: This questions asks for reasons why a teacher should join the BCS – for six marks, three reasons are needed.

Question 2: This is a contextual question – for six marks, three disadvantages are required.

Protecting data

Specification reference

3.3.6h – discuss how encryption, authorisation, authentication, virus checking, virus protection and physical security can be used to protect data.

🔑 Keyword

Data: raw facts and figures, represented by alphanumeric characters. Unprocessed information – without context, structure or meaning.

Weblink

http://computer.howstuffworks. com/encryption.htm

How encryption works.

🖝 Key points to remember

- There is no need to understand how the techniques work, just how they can be used.
- Some techniques prevent data being intercepted, others prevent data being understood.

■ Encryption

This takes plain text and uses an algorithm to convert it into ciphertext (encrypted **data**). A key is then used to decipher the text and turn it back into plain text.

Encryption does not prevent data being intercepted or acquired, it stops it from being understood. It protects the data as the contents cannot be read and used by anyone who does not have the key.

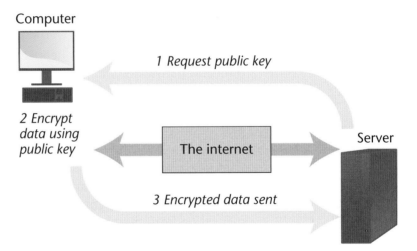

Computer

1 Request public key

2 Encrypt data using public key

The internet

Server

3 Encrypted data sent

RSA encryption

■ Authorisation

This gives an individual or a computer permission to access data. For example, individuals can be authorised to access certain files on a computer. This authorisation can be verbal or written. If someone who is not authorised tries to access the files, they are breaking the Computer Misuse Act 1990. Authorisation given to an individual can be implemented through the use of access rights allocated to their username.

Computer authorisation allows only a certain machine to access a resource. This may be further limited by time restrictions. iTunes uses authorisation to limit the number of computers that can play content from the iTunes store.

Guards and cameras can inform what is happening and may act as a deterrent but will not prevent theft

Authentication

This ensures that the person or computer who is requesting information is who they say they are. This can be done through the use of a key, code word or pin known only to both parties. Authentication is often combined with authorisation.

Virus checking and virus protection

There are two different aspects to viruses. Prevention – stopping a **virus** getting onto a machine in the first place and virus checking – scanning a computer to find any viruses that are on the machine and getting rid of them.

Viruses can perform a variety of tasks – they can remove security from a computer, transfer data from a computer and exploit software insecurities to allow access to a computer.

Creators of viruses and anti-virus software manufacturers are constantly trying to create software which will defeat the other. A new virus is immediately followed by an update to anti virus software to eliminate it.

Physical security

Physical security that prevents access to data includes the use of locked doors and **biometric** security. Computers can be locked to the floor or a desk so that they cannot be taken.

Exam questions

1 Describe how encryption can be used to protect data.

[*4 marks*]

2 Explain measures that can be used to prevent viruses causing a security breach. [*6 marks*]

Examiner hints and tips

Think about the following in relation to the above questions.

Question 1: This question requires a learnt response on encryption. Do not describe how encryption works – this is not necessary, but focus on how it can protect data.

Question 2: This question is looking for answers related to preventing viruses and removing viruses.

6.8

Hardware and software developments

Specification reference

3.3.6i – discuss hardware and software developments that are changing, or might change, the way we live. Examples might include advances in treating injuries or disease, leisure activities, the environment, the home, education and freedom of speech and movement. This list of examples is not exhaustive as questions will reflect the current use or abuse of ICT in society.

Keyword

Future developments in ICT: these include hardware, software or different uses for equipment. They do not have to be futuristic but must be recent.

Weblink

http://www.wired.co.uk/

Up-to-date news and discussions on ICT.

Key points to remember

- Look at the chapter on answering questions – the discussion is as important as the content.
- Read newspapers and watch television news – keep up to date with developments in ICT.

The final question on the examination paper is likely to be an essay related to the second key point. You are expected to be up to date in **future developments in ICT** and to express your own opinion. You need to be able to understand and write about the consequences and impacts of the introduction of new developments.

Future developments of ICT

ICT is constantly evolving – hardware, software and how the technology is used. The specification identifies key areas – treating injuries or disease, leisure activities, the environment, the home, education and freedom of speech and movement. These have been provided to give you topics to research. They are not the only topics that you may be asked about. The exact nature of the answer is up to you – decide what areas of those topics you are familiar with and wish to discuss. Some ideas have been given below for each topic – you would need to develop positive and negative impacts and consequences of these to get high marks on the final question on the paper.

Treating injuries or disease

This could include the use of ICT in research, remote surgery, robotics, expert systems for diagnosis, creating medical components, biometrics and androids.

Leisure activities

This could include the use of virtual reality to experience a holiday, games machines, advances in cinematography (Avatar, for example), theme park rides (design and control), mobile technology and music devices.

Weblinks

http://news.bbc.co.uk/1/hi/ technology/default.stm

BBC technology and clickbits website for keeping up to date with ICT developments.

http://www.btplc.com/Innovation/ News/timeline/index.htm

BT Technology Timeline 2006–2051.

◼ The environment

This could include the use of technology to reduce CO_2 emissions (in cars and houses), plot the best route for a delivery vehicle to minimise fuel consumption, sense and forecast weather using satellites and to save energy.

◼ The home

There are many developments here – fridges, cookers, lawn mowers and vacuum cleaners have been updated with technology; as have sound, water, heating and security systems within the house. The use of biometrics in the home and computer control are both topics.

◼ Education

ICT in education includes the use of online tutoring and testing. ICT in the classroom includes the use of mobile devices, teleconferencing and software. ICT can be used for online marking and submissions, plagiarism software (to see if you have copied from the internet) and the provision of materials (books, 3D modelling and sound/video and different methods of utilising it – for example, electronic readers).

◼ Freedom of speech and movement

This includes monitoring convicted criminals using CCT, implanted chips or iPhones and using software to track travel and collect information on movement (through items such as purchases, passports and cameras).

There are issues of privacy and how the data collected is used – some question the ethics of collecting information about people; others say what is the harm if they are innocent.

Exam questions

1 Discuss the impact of new hardware and software developments on the use of devices in the home . [*11 marks*]

2 Discuss the impact of new hardware and software developments on monitoring an individual's personal freedom. [*11 marks*]

Examiner hints and tips

Think about the following in relation to the questions on the left.

Question 1: Your answer needs to focus on the positive and negative impacts and consequences of the use of hardware and software devices in the home. The impacts and consequences can be for the individual or environment.

Question 2: Impacts can be negative, for example, tracking movements and online existence or positive, for example, reducing crime.

6.9 Confidentiality of data

Specification reference

3.3.6g – discuss the need to keep data confidential and explain how this can be achieved.

 Keyword

Confidential: only revealed to those who need to know – keeping it secret.

Weblink

http://www.microsoft.com/protect/ fraud/passwords/checker.aspx

Password strength checker.

Key point to remember

■ Data needs to be kept confidential to comply with the Data Protection Act 1998 and for competitive advantage.

The Data Protection Act 1998 requires personal data to be kept secure. This is one of the reasons why a company needs to ensure that data is **confidential**. The second reason is competitive advantage – if another company was to get hold of the information it could undercut them, bring products out earlier and beat them to the market, potentially causing them to go bust.

How is data kept confidential? One way is to restrict access. This can be done by the use of passwords, access rights and physical security. These methods can prevent individuals getting to the data.

Another method is encryption – even if the data is accessed, it cannot be understood. Staff should be educated to not leave their computer unlocked, not give out their password or data about people and follow rules on attachments, malware and viruses.

A company can run and update anti virus software and install a firewall between the intranet and internet. They can also authorise workstations and set time limits on access.

For passwords, three strikes and the account is locked and password rules can be applied. Password rules include not reusing old passwords, minimum password length, using non-dictionary or personal words and inclusion of a capital letter, lowercase letter and a number. Following these rules will reduce the chance of the password being guessed.

Exam questions

1 Explain why data needs to be kept confidential. [4 marks]

2 Explain how a company can ensure a password is as strong as possible. [6 marks]

Examiner hints and tips

Think about the following in relation to the questions on the left.

Question 1: This question asks for the reasons why data must be kept confidential. The two reasons are legal and competition – expand and make sure you say why.

Question 2: This question is about the rules that a company can apply. You need to say what the rules are and how they improve security.

Examination techniques

■ Types of examination questions and how to answer them

All the examination questions include a keyword such as 'identify' or 'describe'. You must recognise these and respond correctly. These words determine what you are required to do to be awarded the allocated marks.

State or identify

Here, you have to write a single word or phrase.

Example

> **1** Identify three different methods for installing a new computer-based information system. [*3 marks*]

Your answers only need to be single words:

> *Pilot, direct and parallel.*

Describe

These types of questions are moving to a higher level of difficulty. These questions are usually worth at least two marks. You need to provide an answer that matches the question asked, using the given context. As a rule of thumb, try to give an example related to the scenario.

Look at the number of marks awarded and divide by two. This is the number of points you should be making. For example:

Example

> **2** Describe change management factors that should be considered when introducing a new ICT system. [*6 marks*]

Six divided by two equals three. You should be looking at making a minimum of three different descriptions.

Remember a good description might earn extra marks in some questions. Take your time in thinking about these questions and preparing what you will write.

The rule of thumb is that in order to answer a description, you need to give an identification (worth one mark) and then go on to say something more about what you have identified – this is known as amplification. Wherever possible, using an example related to the context is also a good idea – this is known as exemplification.

Identify, amplify and exemplify.

Example

3 Describe the facilities of a discussion board for seeking customer feedback on a new product. [*4 marks*]

You need to first identify the features that you are going to talk about, then give some more information and, finally, give an example in context:

Threads – this is where a message is posted and a second message posted and linked to the first one. It can include quotes from the previous message. A user can visit a thread and see all the relevant posts. Threads allow messages on the same topic to be kept together.

Notification of new posts – if a new message is posted then the system can send en email letting the users know. This can contain the text of the message as well, such as a review of a product.

Explain

These types of questions usually require you to provide either advantages or disadvantages. This is a description with a reason. Your answer must be written in continuous prose. These questions are usually worth two marks.

An explanation is an identification, followed by amplification and example (the description), followed by the reason why it is an advantage/disadvantage. The reason should be contextualised.

Example

4 Explain how user perception can be used in the design of a user interface for a booking system. [*2 marks*]

Your answer needs to include a reason, followed by the advantages of that reason:

The system needs to follow the order that the user expects. If the user is expecting it to have an order similar to a manual or phone booking, and it matches that order, then they will think they know how to use the interface and find it easier to use. The manual system can be used as the basis for the design of the interface.

Compare

To answer these type of questions, you will need to identify a feature that you are comparing and then apply that feature to both things being compared. If you are asked to compare, you must include both sides of the comparison. This question will usually be worth three marks – it will require three comparisons, one mark per comparison.

Example

5 Compare the characteristics of a LAN and a WAN. [*2 marks*]

Your answer will need to identify a feature/item and give an explanation of how a LAN and a WAN deal with that feature. A writing frame has been used to ensure a proper comparison is made – these are notes:

Item/feature	LAN	WAN
Internal/external	Available to all computers internally. If external access – known as an extranet.	External to the organisation, uses telecommunications links.
Ownership	All components owned by organisation.	Uses items owned by other people.

You then need to write your answer in continuous prose. Make sure it is clear that you have made a comparison. Use words such as: 'whereas', 'and', 'but'.

A LAN is internal to an organisation, all computers within the organisation can access resources on the LAN, whereas a WAN is external to the organisation which means your computer does not have to be connected within the organisation in order to use the facilities.

In a LAN, all the components used are owned by the organisation itself, this includes all the cables and wireless technology used to make the connections. In a WAN, the equipment used is owned and maintained by a third party – this can include the cables or satellite technology used to transfer the data.

This is a high level of response and requires a significant amount of writing to gain the marks.

Discuss

These type of questions require an explanation that reachs a conclusion. You need to identify a point, identify the impacts of that point and then follow those impacts, through consequences, to logical conclusions.

For a good discussion essay you should be looking at both points of view/sides of the discussion. These should be given as positives/negatives or advantages/disadvantages.

Your essay should end with a conclusion. Make sure you reach a specific conclusion and include phrases such as 'In conclusion…', 'Overall…', 'On balance…'. Your conclusion should be a shortened summary of the main points with a reason for opting for one side over the other.

To move from a point to an impact to a consequence – look at the examples below:

Example

6 Discuss hardware and software developments that have an effect on personal privacy.

Answer	Commentary
GPS devices that are implanted in each individual allow that person to be tracked and their location known at all times.	■ This is the identification of one point that will be discussed.
A signal can be given off that contains a unique identifier and software can monitor and track that individual's location.	■ This is the description – how GPS can work to track individuals is expanded.
Having a location known at all times can be beneficial. If you are involved in an accident when hill walking, for example, a GPS location can help rescue services identify where you are and get help to you. You may be in an area where there is no mobile signal and inclement weather and not be able to contact anyone. The GPS will allow your location to be identified and for you to be found and rescued before further injury, such as hypothermia or even death could occur. This could lead rescue parties straight to you, meaning that there will not be any wasted time searching for you – this can ensure that the budget is used to greater effect as expensive tracking and locating equipment held by the rescue services is not required. The money can be spent on other services.	■ They are going to give a positive impact – that of being able to be located in an accident. ■ This is the why and how the GPS locater is useful and could be used – contextualised with an example. ■ This targets rescue services in particular and starts to tie the impacts into the consequences.
The GPS locator allows an individual's personal privacy to be invaded but for their benefit – that of saving their life.	■ This paragraph ends with the consequences to personal privacy.

This answer gives a positive impact and consequences. For high marks, a negative impact and consequences would also need to be given.

Tip: choose one positive and one negative point. Write at least half a side on each point. Do not be tempted to stray and write about different points in the same paragraph. Make sure you give the point, the impacts of the point and the consequences of that impact.

The essay only needs two points – one positive and one negative (giving more points will increase your chances in case you do not fully develop one of them) – and, ideally, a reasoned conclusion.

Make sure that you develop each point to its logical conclusion. Think about standing in front of your teacher and reading out your essay. If you reach the end of your point and start on a new paragraph, is your teacher going to be waiting for the ending or will they be awarding the mark?

General examination tips

The examination is the end point that all the preparation has been leading up to. You really do need to be prepared, to have put the revision in, looked over past questions and understand how to answer different types of questions. You then stand much more chance of giving answers that will be awarded marks.

The paper is broken into two sections. Section A contains knowledge-based short questions. These should be easy marks for you. Section B contains longer questions set within a context – you must give examples in your answers that relate to the context of the question.

Focus on the question you are answering

Forget the last question and the next section. Concentrate on reading the current question and structuring the best answer you can, making sure to match the key word and the marking scheme.

One mark per minute

If a question is worth two marks then do not spend more than two minutes writing the answer. Sometimes candidates' answers go into too much detail. This means that later answers are rushed and marks are lost due to wasted time. The identify/state questions require short and sharp answers – they are usually knowledge-focused – so get them out of the way quickly.

Find a relaxation point

During the examination you will need to give your brain, back and eyes a brief rest. Look at the clock or a point at some distance just to relax for 30 seconds or so. Do not look around the room as this will distract others and interrupt your thought processes.

No crossing out

If an answer has been crossed out, it does not get marked. If you do not cross the answer out then it will be marked and may still get credit. Only cross an answer out if the question is worth one mark as only the first response will be marked.

Always read carefully what you have written

Read through your answers and make sure you have written exactly what you need to say. The words used and their order can make a difference, so take care. You need every mark. Does the examiner need to add anything to your answer to make sense? If so, then you need to add some more. Add one more example in your response if it is appropriate. Take that bit of extra time to think about your answer before you start to write.

The coursework for OCR A2 ICT is worth 40 per cent of the whole A2 level and is marked out of 80. The coursework is your own choice. It should be based on a problem to solve. You need a client (or someone who is prepared to act as a client). Their involvement is paramount throughout the life of the project.

All through the project you need to keep an activity log. This needs to be filled out each time you do something on the coursework or receive letters or emails. It does not have to be detailed, but should be continuous, from the beginning of the project to the end.

Date	Description
12/12/09	Sent letter to client asking to agree date for interview.
15/12/09	Received letter from client agreeing to interview date.
20/12/09	Interviewed client. Wrote up transcript of interview.

Example of part of an activity log

■ Definition, investigation and analysis

The project begins with a problem being given by the client. This can be very general and is used as a starting point for the investigation. Some background to the company/organisation is needed – what does it do, how many people does it employ, where is it based and how long has it been trading are useful questions to answer. An organisation chart is useful as is identifying who the client is and their place in the hierarchy.

The next step is to collect information about the current system. This has two aims: to confirm and add detail to the problem and to find out what the new system needs to do. You need to decide on the method used to collect information about the current system and justify your choice. Marks are awarded for your planning. You should think about:

- What questions are to be asked.

- Reasons for asking questions.

- Possible follow-up questions for some of them.

- Evidence of communication with the client to arrange the collection of information.

You need to make sure that you are collecting information from all relevant parties – this is usually all the people in the organisation chart. Documents sent to other people, for example, invoices sent to customers are also included. It may be necessary to ask different people or groups of people different questions. If so, these questions need reasons and possible follow-ups as well.

Having planned the data collection, you need to actually collect the data. The evidence required will depend on the method, transcripts, documents, letters, etc. – these all need recording in the project. A transcript does not need to be word for word, it can be a summary of each response.

There needs to be some additional collection of information – this could be looking at documents, observation, questionnaires or additional interviews. You need to justify the method you are using for the additional data collection, collect the information and then present the findings. This could be in graphical form or a written summary.

Having collected all the information you are now in a position to restate the problem – this may be the same as the problem that was originally given, but is more likely to be a refinement. This redefinition needs to be agreed with the client (usually by letter).

The most important document that comes out of the previous data collection is the requirements specification. This is the list of what the final product will do. It is best to keep it specific, for example,

Store customer details,   ✗

Store customer forename, surname, address, email and mobile number.   ✓

The requirements specification should cover everything that the solution will do. Everything that is included in the requirements specification must come from the data collection. There should not be any requirements from the client or users that cannot be justified.

The requirements specification should be agreed by the client – a letter is the best method.

Having agreed the requirements specification, the next step is to look at alternative solutions and decide, in conjunction with the client, the one that should be used. You need three different solutions. These will depend on the type of project you are doing. For a record system, you might compare the use of the existing paper system, a spreadsheet and a database. Compare the three alternative solutions against the requirements specification to see if they can meet them and also against cost and feasibility. You need to come to a reasoned conclusion and this should be signed off by the client.

The final element of analysis is to list the software and hardware required to deliver all the required elements of the solution. The exact list will depend on the project and the requirements it needs to fulfil. It is easier to start by detailing all the software required. Knowing the software will give you the minimum hardware specification required. You may need to increase this and add additional hardware. All software and hardware listed needs to be justified.

Design

The involvement of the client is paramount to the design. They need to comment on all designs that they will use – for example, forms, reports, web pages. They do not need to comment on anything that they will not see – tables, queries, formulae, for example.

The philosophy of the design should be such that a third party could pick it up and create it without needing to ask any questions. Everything needs to be designed. The nature of the project will determine what 'everything' is as it will differ between projects using different applications.

The key to a successful design is completeness and consistency. It must include everything and it must meet the requirements specification. There should be nothing in the design that the client has not agreed to in the requirements specification and everything the client wants should be included.

When designing, you should think about covering the following, as appropriate to the solution you are developing:

1 Input (user interface).

2 Processing (queries, functions and formulae).

3 Output (forms, reports, web pages).

4 Files and data structures (storage).

5 Error messages.

6 Security and access rights.

You will need specification designs, layout designs and structure designs for the different elements.

The last element of design is the project plan. The project plan covers the creation and testing of the solution. This is a sequential guide to when everything should be created and predecessor tasks. A predecessor task is something that needs to be done before the task can be done.

Task number	Task	Date started	Date ended	Predecessor
1	Create table of customers	12/01/10	12/01/10	
2	Create table of suppliers	12/01/10	12/01/10	
3	Create table of products	12/01/10	12/01/10	2
4	Create table of orders	12/01/10	12/01/10	1
5	Create table of order items	12/01/10	12/01/10	3, 4

In the example above, the table of products cannot be created until after the table of suppliers has been created. This is because the table of products needs a link to the supplier. The 'create table of suppliers' is, therefore, a predecessor task.

When creating the project plan, try and think of every single feature that appears in the design – all of these should be included.

Software development, testing and installation

The first element is to create a test plan. The test plan should test all the elements of the requirements specification as well as any validation you have applied and anything else that is relevant.

The test plan should follow the structure:

ID	Description	Type	Data used	Expected output

Make sure that the data used is specific and you have all types of test – valid (normal), invalid (erroneous) and extreme (boundary). You should also consider navigation and end-user testing.

The next part of this section is to provide evidence of some developmental testing. When you create your solution, there will be elements that you test as you develop – queries, formulae, etc. – usually the processing elements. You need to provide informal evidence of this testing – a description of the testing, data used, any problems and resolutions.

Having created the solution, you need to provide evidence. This is done by taking screenshots of everything that has been created. You need to show data structures, processing, formulae/functions, queries, reports, macros, validation – everything printed and annotated.

One area that needs specific evidence is the interface. You need to show how you have customized the interface to meet the requirements of the end user – for example, how you have adapted the software to meet the house style.

Having documented your solution, you now need to provide evidence of testing. Take the test plan and run the tests. Make sure that you provide output for the tests, cross-referenced against the ID number of the test. If any tests fail, show how you resolved the issue and document the retest.

The final part of this section is installation. You do not have to install the system but you do have to plan for the installation of the system. There are three sections that need covering: user training; files, hardware and software; and method of changeover.

You need to give details on the training that will be required and, if necessary, when and how this training will take place. The dates of training need to be agreed with the client and the timing appropriate to the method of changeover. You need to consider the data that will be used for training purposes and how this will be created/entered.

The system that you have created will require either new data to be entered or existing data to be transferred. There needs to be an indication given of the volume of data that is to be transferred/entered and an estimate as to the time it will take. You also need to give information on when it will take place and who will be doing it.

The organisation may not have the hardware and software required for the new system in place. It may be necessary to upgrade or purchase new hardware and software. The hardware and software required needs to be detailed along with the dates when it is required to be delivered and installed.

You must detail the different methods of changeover, with advantages and disadvantages, in such a way that the client can make a decision. There must be evidence of client consultation and evidence of an informed choice being made and communicated to you by the end user.

The installation plan should contain a calendar of dates which, along with the plan itself, needs to be agreed with the end user.

Documentation

The user guide is for the end user and should detail how to use the system that you have created and not how to use the underlying software or system.

The user guide will contain different sections:

Getting started – this section contains information for the basic user on how to start using the system. It should contain the purpose of the software and all the basic information required to use the system. It should also detail if a username and password are needed and, if so, where they are obtained from.

User guide – this is the most important of all of the sections. It contains all the information needed to run the system on a day-to-day basis. It needs to contain details on entering data, processing, outputs, backup and recovery of data.

Different projects will have different individuals as the end user – a website, for example, is unlikely to have a paper guide for the user of the website but, if it contains a back end database, then it will have a paper guide for the use of that part of the project.

Troubleshooting – this is a guide to problems and solutions and needs to list all the different problems the user might encounter, what caused them and how to overcome them. Any error messages the system generates must be included.

Online help – the online help will depend on the package you are using. It could be web-based help using HTML, a collection of tool tips or a series of text files accessed by a button click.

Evaluation

It is not possible to achieve marks in this section unless you have completed the requirements specification earlier in the project. To complete the evaluation, you need to take each objective listed in the requirements specification and discuss the degree of success you have had in meeting it. It is not important whether you meet all of the objectives. You can still achieve full marks for this section even if you have not managed to complete all the objectives.

The evaluation must include comments from the end user/client, which should be backed up with evidence from the report. The focus needs to be on the requirements. Is the end user satisfied that the system does everything that it should do?

The evaluation should include shortfalls in the system and any extensions to the system and how they will be carried out. Shortfalls in the system are areas where you have not met the requirements specification and the system fails to achieve its objectives. There may not be any shortfalls in your system – if this is the case, then this section does not need to be completed. If there are shortfalls, then they need to be identified and methods given for correcting them, so that they are eliminated. There is no requirement to carry out the correction.

Possible extensions – you must not only describe the possible extensions but give some idea as to how to carry them out. This does not need to be a complete design, but a very general description of what might be done to implement the extension.

This section requires the use of your imagination. You need to think about what you would do to improve the new system. Some of the suggestions might already be in your project, in which case you will need to think further afield.

■ Presentation

Marks are awarded for the presentation of your entire coursework. Your project should include detailed and accurate means of navigation – this means a title and contents page. The contents page should map the different sections and headings of the project. Presentation needs to be consistent and to use an appropriate font size and font style.

The intended audience is your teacher and the moderator. The order of your project should be the same as the order of marking. The user must be presented as a stand-alone document to gain high marks.

Spelling and grammar errors in the report should be as few as possible and it should finish with a copy of the log of events, which should be logically correct. Dates on letters in the project and the project plan should correspond with the log of events.

Index